McCallum's Writing Glossary

Aber Creative Writing Guides
The Business of Writing
The Craft of Fiction
Ghost Writing
Writing Crime Fiction
Kate Walker's 12 Point Guide to Writing Romance
Writing Historical Fiction
Writing How-to Articles and Books
Writing TV Scripts
Starting to Write
Writing Soap
Writing Science Fiction
Writing and Imagery

Aber Self-Help
Choose Happiness: Ten Steps to Put the Magic Back into your Life
Write yourself well: How writing therapy can help to cure emotional and physical pain

Aber Money Management
Understanding the numbers: the first steps in managing your money
Back to the Black: How to get out of Debt and Stay out of Debt

McCallum's Writing Glossary

Chriss McCallum BA (Hons)

Chriss McCallum

Aber publishing

© 2011 Chriss McCallum
© 2011 Cover Design Aber Publishing

ISBN 978-1-84285-114-2

This edition is published by Aber Publishing
Aber Publishing is a division of GLMP Ltd

Website://www.aber-publishing.co.uk

NOTE: The material contained in this book is set out in good faith for
general guidance and no liability can be accepted for loss or expense
incurred as a result of relying in particular circumstances on statements
made in this book. Laws and regulations are complex and liable to change
and readers should check the current position with the relevant authorities
where appropriate.

Author's Note

My thanks to award-winning poet Alison Chisholm, author of 'Crafting Poetry' (Lulu.com, Amazon.com) for generously giving permission for her poems to be included as examples on pages 22, 23, 62, 101, 101–2.

Usually books are set using Hart's Rules which clearly state that book titles should be set in italic. Since I have deliberately used italic to help you cross-reference terms, this is not the case in this book. My purpose has been to help you learn the terms involved in writing and book production and it was therefore felt that setting book titles correctly may lead to confusion.

Introduction

To become a professional writer in today's fiercely competitive publishing world, you need more than hard work and a talent for writing. You need to know the language of the business, so that you can talk with agents, editors and publishers on an equal footing, confident that you understand the terms they use and how those terms apply to the work you offer them.

This book gives you the knowledge you need. With cross-references set in italics, here are concise explanations of

- publishing terms and jargon
- printing terms
- literary and popular fiction forms
- poetry and verse forms, with examples
- basic Internet and digital terms.

Familiarity with these terms will also enable you to recognise and avoid the sharks who lurk in the shallows of publishing, tempting the unwary writer with 'vanity' deals that can empty your pockets and ruin your reputation.

Whatever your chosen field, be it novels, short stories, poetry, articles or non-fiction books, the knowledge and confidence you'll gain from this book will give a huge boost to your chances of professional success. Enjoy the journey.

Chriss McCallum
chriss.mccallum@aber-publishing.co.uk

Glossary

A

A3: see *paper sizes*.

A4: see *paper sizes*.

A5: see *paper sizes*.

AA: *abbr* of *author's alteration*.

abbr: see *abbreviation*.

abbreviation (*abbr* abbr): *n* a short form of a word.

abridgement: *n* the shortening of a work, often done by cutting out descriptive passages and, possibly, minor *characters(1)*. (Old French: 'shorten'.)

abstract: *n* a *synopsis* of a *piece* of *non-fiction* writing. (Latin: 'drawn out'.)

academic publishing: *n* the production of books and *journals* for higher education.

accent: *n* a mark placed above or below a letter to show how it should be pronounced. (Latin: 'like a song'.)

acceptance: *n* an offer from an *editor* to publish submitted work; a few *markets(1)* offer *payment on acceptance* but most pay after (sometimes long after) *publication(1)*.

acknowledgements: *n* intimations of thanks for help received from individuals and/or other *publications(2)*.

acquisitions/acquiring editor: see under *editor*.

Acrobat: see *Adobe Acrobat Reader*.

acronym: *n* a word formed from the initial letters or *syllables* of other words, *eg* RADAR (radio detection and ranging).

acrostic: *n* a short *verse* form in which the first letters of the lines – or, rarely, the last letters – when read consecutively, form a word or a letter pattern (ABC etc). (Greek: 'end of verse-lines'.)

act: *n* a division of a play or an opera, often sub-divided into *scenes*.

action tag: *n* a mini-*characterisation*; *eg* 'the old man shuffled across the road'.

Active Server Pages (*abbr* ASP): *n* technology that lets *web* designers place *scripts(2)* inside a *web page*, those scripts being activated by the *web server* before the *page* is sent to the user.

active voice: *n* the use of *verbs* that 'make things happen'; *eg* 'Tom chased Jerry' is active and thus stronger than 'Jerry was chased by Tom'. See also *passive voice*.

adage: *n* a *proverb* or saying. (Latin: 'saying'.)

adaptation: *n* conversion of an existing work into a different form for another medium; *eg* a *novel* into a play.

addendum: *n* 1. material printed separately at the beginning and/or end of a book, supplementary to the main content. 2. additional *copy* attached to a *manuscript page* to be *taken in* where indicated on that page.

adhesive binding: see *perfect binding*.

adjective (*abbr* adj): *n* a word preceding a noun to qualify its meaning, *eg* 'big' 'small', 'pretty', 'ugly'.

adjudicator: *n* a person who acts as a judge in a competition in one of the arts.

Adobe Acrobat Reader: *n* free *software* which allows you to read *downloaded files*.

adoption: *n* a book recommended for use in schools, colleges or universities.

ADSL: see *Asymmetric Digital Subscriber Line*.

adult fiction: *n fiction* which might be sexually explicit.

advance: *n* money paid to an *author* in advance of *publication(1)* on account of *royalties* on future book sales. Under the usual terms the *publisher* will retain the author's royalty until the advance is paid off, after which the author receives his or her agreed share of the revenue (usually net or actual revenue); the advance is usually paid in instalments, part when the *contract* is signed, part on delivery of an acceptable *manuscript*, and possibly part on publication. An advance is not normally subject to repayment even if the book does not sell well enough to reimburse the publisher.

advance copy: *n* a copy of a book, possibly in *page proof* form, sent out to reviewers and *publishers'* representatives before *publication(1)* in the hope of generating advance publicity and/or orders.

Advance Information sheet (*abbr* AI sheet): *n* a publicity *document* giving sales and marketing information about a book, issued by the *publisher* before *publication(1)*.

advance order: *n* a sales order obtained by a *publisher* before *publication(1)*, on the strength of a book's *title(1)*, subject, cover and/or its *author*'s reputation.

adventure: *n* a *genre* of *fiction* in which action is more important than *characters(1)* or *theme*.

adverb (*abbr* adv): *n* a word which modifies the meaning of a *verb*; *eg* 'quietly'.

advertisement: *n* publicity that is paid for.

advertorial: *n text(1)* in a *magazine* which is not written by staff but by an advertiser; the words 'advertising feature' usually appear at the top of the *page*.

advice column: *n* a *regular feature* offering advice about *readers'(1)* problems.

adware: *n software* that tracks your *web* use and delivers *advertisements* relevant to your interests direct to your *e-mail* address.

aesthetics: *n* the philosophical study of the nature of beauty. (Greek: 'things perceptible to the senses'.)

affectation: *n* a false or pretentious *style* of writing, unsuitable for its subject and/or its *readership*. (Latin: 'aspiration'.)

afterword: *n* 1. material about a work or its *author* added after the main *text(1)*. 2. a concluding section by a work's *author*.

age banding: *n* a guide to the reading age to which a *publisher* considers a book best suited; sometimes printed on the covers of children's books. (Disliked by many *authors* and library services, who feel this kind of description might discourage buyers and *readers(1)*.)

agent: see *literary agent*.

aggregator: see *news aggregator*.

agony column: *n* a regular *magazine feature* offering advice on (usually emotional) problems.

agreement: see *contract*.

AI sheet: see *Advance Information sheet*.

AIDA: Attention, Desire, Interest, Action; a mantra for writing sales *copy*.

air: *n* the white space on a printed *page*.

airport edition: *n* a *paperback edition* of a new book which might be on sale at airports before its official *publication date*.

aka: *n acronym* for 'also known as'.

alazon: *n* a stock *character(1)* in Greek comedy, a self-deceiving boastful impostor. See also *eiron*.

alexandrine: *n* in *poetry*, a line of six *iambic feet*; so-called because some early French poems about Alexander the Great were written in this *metre*.

alignment: *n* the accurate levelling of *characters(2)* and words in a line of *text(1)*.

all rights: *n* the right to publish, broadcast, adapt or exploit a work in any form. See also *rights* and *copyright*.

allegory: *n* a *narrative* which not only makes complete sense in its own action, *characters(1)*and *setting(2)* but also has a symbolic significance. (Greek: 'speaking otherwise'.)

alley: *n* white space between two *columns(1)* of *text(1)*.

alliteration: *n* two or more words that begin with the same sound; *eg* 'wild winter wind'. (Latin: 'more letters'.)

allusion: *n* a reference, either explicit or indirect and usually brief, to a person, place, event, or another literary work. (Latin: 'to play with'.)

almanac(k): *n* a calendar or register of the days, weeks and months of a year, listing anniversaries, astronomical events *etc*.

alpha hero: *n* in *romantic fiction*, a *hero* who is super-confident and very much 'in charge'.

alphabet length: *n* the length of the *lower case* letters in a particular *font*.

alteration: see *author's alteration, editorial alteration, printer's error*.

Amazon: *n* the world's leading *Internet bookseller*.

ambience: see *atmosphere*.

ambient media: *pl n* outdoors *advertising*, like posters, billboards, *advertisements* on the sides of buses, in tube, train and bus stations and the like.

ambiguity: *n* the use of a word or expression that could mean more than one thing; might be deliberate, but can result from careless *syntax* or imprecise use of words or *punctuation*. (Latin: 'shifting'.)

American Standard Code for Information Interchange (*abbr* ASCII): *n* a code used for transmitting and storing *text(1)* on computers; also used to describe *text(1)*-only *documents*.

amnesia plot: *n* in *fiction*, a *plot* that centres on a *character(1)* losing or regaining their memory.

ampersand: *n* the *symbol(1)* & representing 'and'.

anachronism: *n* an error in *chronology*, in which something is placed in the wrong period of time; *eg* a *character(1)* using a mobile phone in the 1960s. (Greek: 'refer to a wrong time'.)

anagram: *n* the letters of a word or words mixed up to make another word; *eg* redistribute 'Sherlock Holmes' to get 'Heh – smell crooks'. (Greek: 'writing anew'.)

analogy: *n* a similarity in one or more respects between two things which are otherwise different. (Greek: 'equality'.)

analysis: *n* the dissection of the *structure* of a work. (Greek: 'undo'.) See *critical analysis*, *market study*.

anapaest: *n* in *poetry*, a *foot* consisting of two unstressed *syllables* followed by one stressed syllable; the reverse of a *dactyl*. (Greek: 'reversed'.)

anecdotal article: *n* a light *article* about everyday life.

anecdote: *n* a short *narration* of an enlightening, amusing or curious incident; a verbal *illustration* from life. (Greek: 'things unpublished'.)

angle: *n* 1. treatment of a subject or *story* from a *viewpoint* designed to serve a particular purpose and influence the *reader(1)'s* response. 2. concentration on one aspect of a *topic*.

angle brackets: *n* the signs < and > used in literary *texts(1)*, scientific and mathematical works.

annals: *n* historical records, written yearly; *eg* 'The Anglo-Saxon Chronicle' (9th–12th century). (Latin: 'yearly'.)

anniversary article: *n* an *article* recalling, re-examining or enlarging upon a past event; topics can range from the famous to the local or the long-forgotten, and are featured in *newspapers* and *magazines* on or near the event's anniversary.

annotation: *n* 1. an explanatory note printed in the *margin* beside a *text(1)*. 2. an explanatory note in an *edition* of an established work, *eg* a Shakespeare play. 3. an explanatory note attached to an *illustration*.

annual: *n* a book that is published and/or updated every year.

anonym: *n* a *publication(2)* whose *author* is unknown or unnamed.

anonymous: *adj* of unknown name or authorship. (Greek: 'without name'.)

antagonist: *n* the principal opponent-*character(1)* in a *story*, the main opposition to the *protagonist*. (Greek: 'struggle against'.)

anthology: *n* a collection of *stories, poems, essays etc,* which might or might not have been published before. Could be works by different *authors* or by the same author (in which case the term *collection* is more usual). (Greek: 'flower collection'.)

anthology rights: *n rights* granted to a compiler and/or *publisher* to reproduce *contributors'* work in an *anthology*.

anthropomorphism: *n* the attribution to animals of human characteristics and qualities. (Greek: 'human-form-ism'.)

anticlimax: *n* an unexpected let-down, often ludicrous or disappointing, after a progressive build-up of expectation or *tension*. (Greek: 'down ladder'.)

anti-hero: *n* a leading male *character(1)* who is attractive but who is also capable of behaviour that is less than heroic.

anti-heroine: *n* the female counterpart of the *anti-hero*.

antiquarian book: *n* an old (more than 75 years), rare and *out-of-print* book.

antithesis: *n* the second of two opposed ideas; an argument in opposition to a proposition. (Greek: 'opposite placing'.)

antonym: *n* a word that means the opposite of another word; *eg* the antonym of 'high' is 'low'.

aphorism: *n* a short concise statement containing a general truth; *eg* 'Nothing great was ever achieved without enthusiasm' (Ralph Waldo Emerson, 1803-82).

apocrypha: *pl n* writings of unknown authorship, considered to be not quite valid. (Greek: 'things hidden'.)

apologia: see *apology*.

apology (also *apologia*): *n* a work of justification or vindication in which the *author* justifies his or her beliefs, actions or opinions; might be autobiographical, philosophical, critical or confessional. (Greek: 'defence'.)

apostrophe: *n* a mark ' showing either an omission of a letter or letters, *eg* 'it's' short for 'it is', or the formation of a simple possessive noun, *eg* 'The dog's tail wags when he hears the man's voice.' See also *greengrocer's plural*.

app: see *applications software*.

appendix (*pl* appendices): *n* an additional section following the main *text(1)* of a book, giving supplementary information.

applet: *n* a computer *program* designed to enhance the working of a *web page*.

applications software (*abbr* app): *n computer software* designed to help the user to perform a singular task or multiple related specific tasks.

approval copy: see *inspection copy*.

arabic numerals: *n* the numbers 1, 2, 3, 4, *etc*. See also *Roman numerals*.

arc: *n* the trajectory of a *plot*; describes the rising *tension*, the *climax*, then the descent into the *resolution*.

archaism: *n* an expression no longer in common usage, *eg* 'thine', 'where'er' and the like, which still turn up in *submissions*, especially in *poetry*, and which are unacceptable to *editors* today. (Greek: 'old-fashioned'.)

archetype: *n* a model or prototype: a *story* or *character(1)* in the model of one easily recognised by the *reader(1)*, who then expects, consciously or subconsciously, a similar pattern of story or type of behaviour to the archetypal model; *eg* stories built around a quest often follow the 'Holy Grail' archetype.

archive: *n* 1. a repository of public or company records. 2. a historical *document*. 3. *files* of data stored on *disk*.

art paper: *n* glossy paper suitable for reproducing *illustrations*.

art publisher: *n* a *publisher* who specialises in art books.

article: *n* a factual *piece* dealing with a single subject (or several related subjects).

artwork (*abbr* a/w): *n illustrations*, photographs, ornamental lettering, fancy headings *etc*.

ascender: *n* the part of a *lower case* letter that extends above the height of the letter x, *eg* d, h. See also *descender*.

ASCII: see *American Standard Code for Information Interchange*.

ASP: see *Active Server Pages*.

.asp: *n* the extension used with *Active Server Pages files*.

assignment: *n* a request from an editor to a *freelance* to produce material on a specific topic, with *wordage, angle*, fee and possibly a *kill fee* usually being agreed in advance.

assistant editor: see under *editor*.

assonance: *n* harmony of sound, achieved through vowel sounds or combinations of vowel and consonant sounds; *eg* 'slumbering under the sun'; a powerful tool for creating emotional or sensuous effects. (Greek: 'to echo'.)

asterisk: *n* the sign * used as a reference mark.

'as-told-to' article: *n* a factual *article*, usually a *personal experience* or an *opinion piece* written in *first-person narrative* by another person who is given joint *credit*.

Asymmetric Digital Subscriber Line (*abbr* ADSL): *n* a line for permanent high-speed connection to the *Internet*.

atmosphere: *n* the over-all *tone* of a work, especially a *novel*, setting up the *reader(1)'s* expectations about what will happen in the course of the *story*; also called *mood* and *ambience*.

attribution: *n* the stating of sources of quoted material.

auction: *n* in publishing, the selling of books and *rights* by inviting bids.

audio: *n* and *adj* reproduction of recorded or broadcast sound.

audio book: *n* a book produced in *audio format*.

audio stream: *n* sound broadcast through the *Internet*.

audiovisual: *adj* relating to sound and vision.

author: *n* the original creator of a work.

author-illustrator: *n* a person who writes and illustrates his or her own work.

author bio: see *author biography*.

author biography (*abbr* author bio): *n* information about an *author*, including previously published works, often included in an *Advance Information sheet*.

author questionnaire: *n* a form sent to an *author* requesting information about their qualifications and credentials, availability to promote their book, knowledge of markets, access to publicity etc . . . any information that might help sales.

author tour: *n* a tour of different locations made by an *author* to promote their book.

author's alteration (*abbr* AA): *n* any change to *proofs* made by the *author* that goes beyond the correction of *printer's errors*; *ie* an alteration that varies from the original *typescript*. Most *contracts* include provision for a proportion of such alterations to be charged to the *author*.

author's copies: *n* an agreed number of books given free by the *publisher* to the *author* on *publication(1)* of their book.

author's discount: *n* a discount allowed to an *author* enabling them to buy copies of their book at a discounted price, and sometimes to buy other books from their *publisher* at a favourable rate.

author's proofs: *n proofs* sent to the *author* for correction and approval. Correctly, these should have been marked already with any errors found by the *publisher's proofreader* and any editorial queries and alterations. In practice, tight publishing schedules and low staffing levels often mean that the *author* receives an unmarked set of proofs on which they are asked to mark errors found and any necessary *alterations*. The publisher than collates printer's, author's and editorial corrections, which have been marked in different coloured inks so that costs can be fairly apportioned.

authorised biography: see *biography*.

autobiographical novel: a *novel* in which the *author* writes a fictionalised version of their life story, in whole or in part; *eg* Nick Hornby's 1992 novel 'Fever Pitch'.

autobiography: *n* a person's life *story*, written by him- or herself. (Greek: 'self-life writing'.)

auto-correct: *n* a computer facility enabling corrections to be made automatically.

auto-indent: *n* an instruction to the computer to indent *text(1)* automatically.

avant-garde: *n* a military expression describing writers and artists who produce work considered to be deliberately experimental and possibly designed to shock. (French: 'before the guard'.)

a/w: *abbreviation* of *artwork*.

B

b&w: *n abbr* of 'black and white', with reference to photographs.

background: *n* the real or imaginary world in which the action of a *story* takes place; includes the physical, emotional and historical factors that relate to that action.

back list: *n* books already published which the *publisher* considers worth keeping *in print*. Also describes a *catalogue* of available books.

back-jacket flap: *n* the part of the printed paper cover that folds inside the back cover on a *hardback*.

back matter: *n* material printed after the main *text(1)* of a book: *appendix, bibliography, glossary, index etc*; also called *end matter*.

back number: *n* a copy of a previous *issue* of a *periodical*.

back of book: *n* the last *pages* of a *magazine*, usually containing *advertisements*.

back story: *n* events that occurred in the *characters'(1)* lives before the action of a *story* began.

back-up copy: *n* a copy on *disk* regularly updated and kept in case of accidents to the working disk; usually stored in a separate place for safety.

bad break: *n* an unsightly break in the *text(1)*; *eg* a clumsily hyphenated word at the end of a line, or the last word of a *paragraph* appearing at the beginning of a *page*.

ballad: *n* a *story* in poetic form, usually *quatrains* in *iambic metre*, with four *feet* in the first and third lines and three feet in the second and fourth lines, *rhyme scheme* abab or abcb; can also mean a romantic song. (French: 'dancing song'.)

balloon: *n* a balloon- or bubble-shaped outline containing words, as used in *cartoons, comic strips, picture-stories etc*.

band rate: *n* the speed at which a *modem* receives data, measured in *bits per second*.

bandwidth: *n* the capacity of a connection to the *Internet* or other communication channel.

bank paper: *n* lightweight paper, thicker than tissue but thinner than *bond*; 45–63 *gsm*.

banner: *n* a *headline* in large *type* extending across the full width of a *newspaper page*.

bar code: *n* a printed machine-readable code in the form of vertical lines.

bard: *n* in Gaelic cultures, a *poet* who celebrates events, particularly heroic deeds; also a common nickname for Shakespeare. (Welsh: 'poet'.)

BASIC: see *Beginner's All-Purpose Symbolic Instruction Code*.

bastard title: see *half-title*.

bathos: *n* unintentional descent from passionate heights to ridiculous depths. (Greek: 'deep'.)

BBC: see *British Broadcasting Corporation*.

BBC Writer's Room: an information source for writers wanting to write for the *BBC*; see www.bbc.co.uk/ writersroom.

BBIP: see *British Books in Print*.

bcc: see *blind carbon copy*.

Beat Generation: *n* a group of American writers working in the 1950s who rejected middle-class American values and looked for truth through drugs, sex, Zen Buddhism and mysticism; included Allan Ginsberg, Jack Kerouac and William Burroughs.

Beginner's All-Purpose Symbolic Instruction Code (*abbr* BASIC): *n* a computer programming language.

'behind the news' information: *n facts* about people involved in and causes behind events in the news, fed in to increase *readers'(1)* understanding of a news *story*.

belles-lettres: *n* elegant literature, including *essays, criticism, literary fiction* and *poetry*; a literary parallel to 'beaux arts'. (French: 'fine writing'.)

Berne Convention: *n* the 1886 International Convention on Copyright; any book copyrighted in any of the countries who signed up to the convention is automatically copyrighted in all the other signatory countries. Some countries, notably the United States of America, did not sign the convention.

bestseller: *n* a book that sells many copies; the word appears widely in *puffs* and/or *blurbs* to help promote sales of a book; the term is often used more in hope than achievement.

beta hero: *n* in *romantic fiction,* a strong, but less tough and unbending male lead than the *alpha hero*.

bf: *abbr* of *bold face*.

B format paperback: *n* a *paperback* with the *format* 198 mm x 129 mm.

bible paper: *n* thin opaque paper used for books with many pages, to keep them light.

biblio page: see *bibliographic page*.

bibliographic page (*abbr* biblio page): *n* a *page* giving details of a book's publishing history, such as *publication date, imprint, copyright* notice, *ISBN etc*; usually printed on the *verso* of the *title page*.

bibliography: *n* a list of books consulted in preparing a work, acknowledging sources of knowledge and *research*. (Greek: 'writing about books'.)

bibliomania: *n* love of books and/or love of collecting books.

bibliophile: *n* a person who loves books.

'big I, the': *n* a derogatory term applied to writing which tends to irritate and alienate *readers(1)* by excessive use of the pronoun 'I'.

bildungsroman: *n* a *novel* describing the *protagonist's* development from childhood to maturity; *eg* James Joyce's 'A Portrait of the Artist as a Young Man' (1916). (German: 'formation-novel'.)

bi-monthly: *n* a *publication(2)* that appears every two months.

biographical dictionary: *n* an alphabetical list of people, giving details of their lives and achievements.

biographical novel: *n* a *novel* in which the *author* presents real people and *backgrounds* in a work of *fiction*, to bring out the truth as he or she sees it; *eg* 'The Master' (2004), Colm Tóibín's novel about Henry James.

biography: *n* an account of a person's life as investigated and evaluated by someone else. An *authorised biography* is written with the approval and possibly the assistance of the subject and/or his or her family and friends. An *unauthorised biography* is written without the consent and possibly against the wishes of the subject and/or family and friends. (Greek: 'life-writing'.)

bit: *n* abbreviation of 'binary digit', the smallest unit of information used in a computer.

'biter-bit' story: *n* usually a *short-short story*, reversing the usual *story* idea in which the *reader(1)'s* sympathies lie with the main *character(1)*. Here, the main character is usually a *villain* who gets their comeuppance as a result of their own actions and/or shortcomings.

bits per inch (*abbr* bpi): *n* a measurement of the density of data on a storage medium.

bits per second (*abbr* bps): *n* the number of *bits* of information that can be passed through telecommunication equipment in one second.

bi-weekly: *n* a *publication(2)* that appears every two weeks.

black letter: see *Gothic(1)*.

black humour: *n* writing that deals in a distorted, nightmarish and cynical way with social problems and social misfits; *eg* Samuel Beckett's play 'Waiting for Godot' (1954).

blad: *n* a sample *booklet*, showing what a book's binding and part of its *text(1)* will look like; used in *promotion*.

blank verse: *n* unrhymed *verse*.

blasphemy: *n* contemptuous or profane reference to God; a criminal offence in the UK.

blind carbon copy (*abbr* bcc): *n* an *e-mail* facility that lets you send the same message to several people at the same time without revealing the list to the other recipients. It comes from the use of carbon paper to make copies when typewriters were in use. Carbon paper was a black or blue inked sheet that went under the main document, and as the letter-key hit the page it simultaneously hit the carbon, thus typing a second copy at the same time.

blind folio: *n* a blank *page*.

blind p: *n* the mark ¶ used to indicate a new *paragraph*.

blockbuster: *n* a book that is particularly 'big', in size, *style* and usually sales, too.

block letter: *n* 1. a heavy-letter *type*, without *serifs*; 2. a *capital letter*.

blog: *n* a *weblog*, an *online* diary. Of particular interest to writers are blogs like those of *eg* ghost-writing specialist Andrew Crofts (http://andrewcrofts.blogspot.com/) and the *BBC Writers Room* blog at http://www.bbc.co.uk/blogs/writersroom/

blogger: *n* a person who writes a *blog*.

blogosphere: *n* the *web* environment where *bloggers* communicate with each other.

blogware: *n software* tools for creating a *blog*.

blow-up: *n* a photographic enlargement.

Bluetooth: *n* technology enabling portable electronic devices like mobile phones to connect with each other and with the *Internet* without the use of wires.

blurb: *n* promotional *text(1)* on a book *jacket* or the back cover of a *paperback*, sometimes exaggerating its worth; (French: 'blah-blah', Spanish: 'bombo'.)

BNB: see *British National Bibliography*.

boards: *n* stiff cardboard covers used in book binding. In a *catalogue*, denotes a *hardcover* binding, probably printed or covered with a decorative picture or pattern, but with no *jacket*.

bodice-ripper: *n* a sexy *novel*, usually historical, disguised as a romance.

body copy: *n* the main *text(1)*, as distinct from *prelims*, *glossary*, *index etc*.

body matter: same as *body copy*.

BOGOF: *n abbr* of the 'Buy one, get one free' selling strategy.

bold/bold face (*abbr* bf): *n type* with a heavy black appearance; indicated in *copy* by wavy underlining.

bombast: *n* turgid and inflated language. (Greek: 'silk'.)

bond paper: *n* good quality paper, usually weighing 70–120 *gsm*.

book club: *n* a society which buys in or prints cheap *editions* for sale to its members.

book club edition: *n* an *edition* of a book produced for sale to *book club* members.

book club rights: *n* the *right* to publish a *book club edition*.

bookfinding service: *n* a service that searches for *out-of-print* or *rare books*.

booklet: *n* a small-*format* book of only a few *pages*, usually *saddle-stitched*.

bookmark: *n* 1. a narrow strip of paper or material used to mark a place in a book. 2. a code used by a *web browser* that lets you return to the same point in the future.

book packager: see *packager*.

bookplate: *n* a label pasted inside a book cover, usually bearing the owner's name.

book proof: *n* a *proof* showing a book's *pages* in the correct order, possibly without *illustrations*.

book review: *n* a critical assessment of a book, usually written when the book is first published.

bookseller: *n* a person who retails books to the public.

book token: *n* a voucher to be used in exchange for books.

Book Trust: *n* formerly the *National Book League*; an independent body which promotes books and reading, and offers an information service.

bookworm: *n* a person who loves reading.

boot: *v* to start up a computer.

bootstrap: *n* the *software* that enables a computer to start up.

border: *n* a continuous ornamental line or design around *text(1)* on a *page*.

born-digital: *adj* describes a *document* that never existed in *hard* copy but which was created and stored in digital form.

box feature: *n* information presented apart from the main *text(1)*; usually marked off with ruled lines. See also *sidebar*.

box head: *n* the heading of a *box feature*.

boxed set: *n* a set of books sold together in a box.

bowdlerise: *v* to remove from a *text(1)* anything that might be remotely offensive; derives from Dr Thomas Bowdler, who 'cleaned up' the works of William Shakespeare in the early 19th century.

brace: *n* the sign } used to connect words, lines, figures, music staves *etc*, indicating that they should be taken together; also called *curly bracket*.

brackets: *n* general name for marks used to enclose words or *symbols(1)*. See *parentheses*.

breach of contract: *n* failure to fulfil the terms of a *contract*.

break-even point: *n* the point at which sales of a book cover its production costs but do not yet show a profit.

break line: *n* the last line at the end of a *paragraph*.

breve: *n* the curved mark ˘ indicating a short vowel or *syllable*.

bridge: see *transition*.

brightener: *n inspirational writing*.

British Books in Print (*abbr* BBIP): *n* a *publication(2)* giving bibliographical details of all books published in the UK.

British Broadcasting Corporation (*abbr* BBC): *n* the United Kingdom's national broadcasting company, a large *market(1)* for writers; see *BBC Writer's Room*.

British National Bibliography (*abbr* BNB): *n* an organisation which publishes a weekly list of all books published in the UK, with monthly and annual *indexes*.

broadband: *n* a continuously open fast connection enabling the use of *Internet*, telephone and *fax* at the same time.

broadcasting rights: *n* the *right* to read or perform work on radio.

broadsheet: *n* a large-*format newspaper*.

brochure: *n* a short, usually unbound, *saddle-stitched* work used for *advertising* or information.

bromide: *n* photosensitive paper used in photography and for the reproduction of *graphic illustrations*.

browser: *n* a *software program* that lets you navigate the *Internet*; *eg* Internet Explorer, Firefox.

bubble: see *balloon*.

budget: *n* a financial plan showing how much money is available and how it is to be used.

bug: *n* an error or defect in a computer *program* or system.

bullet: *n* 1. a large dot • preceding and adding emphasis to an item in a book or *article*; also called a *stab point*. 2. a short piece of information identified by such a dot.

bulletin board: *n* 1. an electronic *database* and discussion *network*. 2. A board on which messages, reminders *etc* can be pinned.

burlesque: *n* a work imitating a serious literary work but making a ridiculous disparity between its *form* and *style* and its subject matter.

burn: *v* to copy data on to a *disk*.

business card: *n* a small printed card bearing a person's name and business details.

business writing: *n copy* written for business *publications(2)*, *eg* company reports, *advertising, newsletters, press releases, catalogues etc*.

buzz word: *n* a word or phrase in current fashion picked up and 'buzzed around' so that it quickly becomes a *cliché*.

byline: *n* a line before or after a *newspaper* or *magazine article*, identifying the writer.

byronic hero: *n* a *hero* of the type portrayed in many *narrative poems* by Lord Byron (1788-1824): a brooding, solitary man, hypnotically fascinating and often concealing some dark secret, *eg* Mr Rochester in Charlotte Brontë's *novel* 'Jane Eyre' (1847).

byte: *n* a measurement of data or memory capacity on a computer.

C

©: a *symbol(1)* signifying that a work is protected by *copyright*.

c & sc: see *capitals and small capitals*.

C sizes: *n* metric paper sizes used for envelopes and folders suitable for paper and stationery in the A sizes (see *paper sizes*); see also *envelope and folder sizes*.

cache: *n* a temporary store of information *downloaded* from the *Internet*.

cadet edition: *n* an *edition* of an adult book 'cleaned-up' for children, *ie* with the rude words taken out.

caesura: *n* a break or pause in a line of *poetry*. (Latin: 'cutting'.)

calligramme: *n* a *poem* written in a particular visual form, using shape and/or areas of space to reinforce its meaning; also called *concrete poetry; eg* George Herbert's 'Easter Wings' (1633), *stanzas* 1 and 2 of 4 (view from the side for the full effect):

Lord, Who createdst man in wealth and store,
Though foolishly he lost the same,
Decaying more and more,
Till he became
Most poore:

With Thee
O let me rise,
As larks, harmoniously,
And sing this day Thy victories:
Then shall the fall further the flight in me.

camera-ready: *adj* describes material ready to be photographed or scanned for printing.

camera-ready copy (*abbr* **CRC**): *n* a typescript which is ready to be photographed or scanned for printing.

canon: *n* a writer's body of work. (Greek: 'rule'.)

canto: *n* a sub-division of a long *poem*.

canzone: *n* mediaeval Italian lyric-style *poetry* with five or six *stanzas* and a shorter final stanza. (Italian: 'a song'.)

cap height: *n* the vertical distance of a *capital* from top to bottom.

capital (*abbr* **cap**): *n* a large letter beginning a sentence or a name; also called an *upper case* letter; indicated on *manuscripts* and *proofs* by three straight lines under the relevant *character(2)*.

capitals and small capitals (*abbr* **c & sc**): *n* a method of *setting(1)* in which words begin with a *capital* letter and the other letters are set in smaller capitals the height of the *lower case* body size. See *small capital*.

caption: *n* a descriptive note printed above, below or beside a picture.

card index: *n* a series of cards for storing information.

careware: *n* *shareware programs* whose fees help good causes.

caret: *n* an insertion mark ^.

caricature: *n* an absurd or exaggerated version. (Italian: 'to load'.)

cartoon: *n* a comic or satirical drawing.

cartoon-strip: *n* a *story* told in a series of *cartoons*, with or without *captions*.

cartouche: *n* a decorative box framing a *text(1)*.

case: *n* the binding of a *hardback*.

casebound: same as *hardback*.

case sensitive: *adj* describes a *program* that can tell the difference between *upper* and *lower case* letters; *eg* 'Poetry' and 'poetry' would be seen as two different words.

cast-off: *n* the calculation of the number of *pages* a piece of *copy* will occupy when *set* in a given size of *type* to a given page area.

catalogue: *n* a list of *publications(2)*.

catalogue verse: *n verse* which lists names of places, people or things.

Cataloguing in Publication (*abbr* **CIP**): *n* a central archiving body to which a *publisher* sends information about forthcoming books; in return, the publisher receives appropriate cataloguing information to include in the *prelims* of his books. In the UK, the national body is the British Library, in America the Library of Congress.

catastrophe: *n* the climax of a *tragedy*, the *dénouement*. (Greek: 'overturning'.)

catchline: *n* an identifying line at the top of a *page* of *typescript* or of a *proof*; discarded when the work is printed; also called a *strap* or *strapline*.

category fiction: *n fiction* written to fit a specific *genre: mystery, romance, fantasy, science fiction* etc.

cause and effect: *n* the essence of *drama* – everything that happens is a cause and every cause has an effect.

cavalier poets: a group of *poets* from the reign of Charles I (1625–49) which included Richard Lovelace (1618–57) and Robert Herrick (1591–1674).

cc: *n abbr* of 'copies'; used in letters, *memos* and *reports* to indicate that identical copies have been sent to named persons.

CD-Rom: see *Compact Disk – Read Only Memory*.

CD-RW: See *Compact Disk – Re-Writable*.

cedilla (also cédille): *n* a mark placed under the letter ç thus, to indicate an 's' sound.

centre: *v* to position centrally in a given *measure*.

centre fold/centre spread: *n* the centre two facing *pages* of a *publication(2)* or of a *signature*.

centre notes: *n* notes placed between *columns(1)* on a *page*.

centre spread: *n* same as *centre fold*.

chain rhyme: *n* a *rhyme scheme* which carries a rhyming sound from one *stanza* to the next.

chapbook: *n* a *booklet* of stories, *poems* and *ballads*, originally sold by itinerant pedlars (chapmen).

chapel: *n* a branch of a trade union in printing and publishing.

chapter: *n* a main division of a book or *document*.

chapter drop: *n* the space between the top of the *page* and the *chapter heading*.

chapter heading: *n* the *title* or number at the beginning of a *chapter*.

chapter opening: *n* the beginning or first *page* of a *chapter*.

chapter title: *n* a *title* at the beginning of a *chapter* showing what you will find therein; general in *non-fiction*, but seldom used in *fiction* nowadays.

character: *n* 1. a participant in the action of a *story*. 2. an individual letter, *numeral* or *punctuation mark*. (Greek: 'distinctive nature'.)

character count: *n* the total number of *characters(2)* in a piece of *copy*; includes letters, *numerals*, hyphens, *punctuation marks* and also the spaces between words, counted as one character each.

character merchandising: *v* the marketing of a *character(1)* (*eg* Mickey Mouse, Postman Pat) in forms additional to the *stories* in which it appears. Character-related merchandise ranges from pencils to T-shirts to wallpaper.

character set: *n* the collection of letters, numbers and *symbols(1)* in a particular *font*.

character trait: *n* a characteristic of personality which distinguishes a *character(1)* from others, making each one individual and memorable.

characterisation: *n* the giving of distinctive qualities and characteristics to *characters(1)* to 'bring them to life'.

chat room: *n* an *Internet* site enabling visitors to 'talk' to each other via *text(2)* messages.

Chaucerian roundel: *n* a poetic form two lines longer than a *triolet*.

cheap edition: *n* the re-issue of an already published book on cheaper paper and with a cheaper binding.

Chicago Manual of Style, The: *n* a book of instructions on spelling, punctuation *etc*, published by the University of Chicago and widely used by American *editors*, printers and *publishers*. The UK equivalent is *New Hart's Rules: The Handbook of Style for Writers and Editors*, published by Oxford University Press.

chick lit: *n* light *romantic fiction* for young women.

'child's-eye' story: *n* a *story* for adult reading, featuring a child as the *key character*.

chiller: *n* a *thriller* that goes beyond the usual limits of the thriller *story* into the chilling and horrific, *eg* stories by Stephen King (1949–).

chronology: *n* a listing of events in chronological order, with dates. A useful aid to writers in avoiding errors in *characters'(1)* ages, dates of events *etc*. Also called *time-line*.

cinquain: *n* an American poetic form of five lines, the lines having two, four, six, eight and two *syllables* respectively; *eg*

I see
a shadow on
my mirror, looking past
reflection, warning winter comes –
my ghost.
(© Alison Chisholm)

CIP: see *Cataloguing in Publication*.

circulation: *n* the total number of copies of a *publication(2)* distributed.

circumflex: *n* the accent ˆ.

circumlocution: *n* talking around a subject rather than going into it. (Latin: 'speaking around'.)

city magazine (*abbr* **citymag**): *n* a *publication(2)* reflecting the interests of the population of a city area.

citymag: *abbr* of *city magazine*.

clarity: *n* the desired meaning conveyed clearly without waffle or *ambiguity*.

classic poetry: *n poetry* which upholds the principles and ideals of beauty characteristic of Greek and Roman art, architecture and literature.

clause: *n* 1. a section of a *contract*. 2. a group of words containing a *noun* and its finite *verb*.

clean copy: *n manuscript* or other *text(1)* that is easy to read and free of errors.

clean proof: *n* a *proof* that is free (or very nearly free) of errors.

clerihew: *n* a comic *verse* form consisting of two rhyming *couplets*, commenting on a person's life or a specific object; *eg*

Cecil B. de Mille
Rather against his will
Was persuaded to leave Moses
Out of the Wars of the Roses.
(*Anonymous*)

cliché: *n* a hackneyed, over-used word, phrase, idea or *plot*; derives from the French for stereotype, a metal plate used for repeated printing. (French: 'stereotype'.)

cliffhanger: *n* a suspenseful happening, usually at the end of a *chapter* or an *episode* in a *serial*; designed to make the *reader(1)* want to find out 'what happens next'. Derives from early film serials, where the *heroine* would be left literally dangling from a cliff or tied to a railway line, to entice the audience back the following week.

climax: *n* the most intense moment in a *story*, when excitement and *tension* are brought to a peak. A *novel* might include several, a *short story* usually has only one. (Greek: 'ladder'.)

clip/clipping: see *cutting(2)*.

clip art: *n* pre-produced *artwork* for use on computers.

clipboard: *n* a function of a word processing *program* that stores material you have cut so that you can then copy it into another part of your work.

cloak-and-dagger novel: *n* a very dramatic *novel* of intrigue and *suspense*.

clogyrnach: *n* a Welsh poetic form relying on syllabic count and *rhyme*, often with midline rhymes; usually has six lines of eight, eight, five, five, three and three *syllables*, *rhyme scheme* aabbba; *eg*

Christmas trees are fascinating
for a kitten, crouched and waiting
to pounce. She pulls claws,
pats mischievous paws
frees baubles,
starts chasing.
(© Alison Chisholm)

close reading: *n* critical examination of a *text(1)*, to identify its meaning and effects and to analyse the ways in which the *author* achieves and conveys these.

close up: *v* an instruction to remove the space between *characters(2)* or lines.

close-up: *n* a photograph taken very close to the subject.

clothbound: *n* same as *hardback*.

club line: *n* the first line of a *paragraph* appearing at the foot of a *page*; see also *orphan*, *widow*.

.co.uk: *n* denotes a United Kingdom commercial *Internet domain*.

co-author: *n* a writer who co-operates with another to create original work.

codex: *n* a collection of early paper and parchment *manuscripts*. (Latin: 'a set of tablets'.)

co-edition: *n* a book produced by two or more *publishers* working with each other and sharing costs and production work.

coffee-table book: *n* a large, glossy, profusely illustrated book intended more for room decoration than for reading.

coincidence: *n* the occurrence of events at the same time or in a strikingly consecutive way, but with no actual connection between them.

collaboration: *n* two or more people working together to produce a work; sometimes published under a single *pseudonym*, *eg* Nikki Gerrard and Sean French, who write mysteries together as 'Nikki French'. Also called *joint authorship*.

collate: *v* to place the *pages* or *sections* of a book in order ready for binding.

collection: *n* a number of works by the same *author* gathered together and published in a single *volume* or series of volumes.

collective: *n* a self-help group of writers, artists and *editors* who jointly publish books and/or *magazines*.

colon: *n* a *punctuation mark* : mainly used to introduce something.

colophon (US logo): *n* 1. a *publisher's symbol(1)* or emblem, usually appearing on the *jacket* and *title page*, and possibly on a book's *spine*. 2. an inscription at the beginning and/or end of a book, giving *title(1)*, printer's name and location, and date of printing. (Greek: 'finishing touch, summit'.)

colour: *n* 1. a particular *slant* or interpretation a writer puts on a subject. 2. descriptive details which 'colour in' background and give depth to a *story*.

column: *n* 1. a vertical section of writing on a *page*. 2. a regular section in a *publication(2)* written by the same person on the same subject or a related series of subjects.

column centimetre/column inch: *n* all the material contained in a one-centimetre or one-inch depth of a *column(1)*; a method of measuring *advertisements*.

columnist: *n* a person who writes a regular *column(2)*.

.com: *n* denotes an American/international *Internet domain*.

comedy: *n* humorous plays, gags, *sketches(2)*, routines *etc* written for performance on stage, radio or television.

comic relief: *n* the use of humorous *characters(1)*, speeches or *scenes* to provide a *counterpoint* to tragic or dramatic events.

comic strip: *n* a series of consecutive adjoining *cartoons* showing a sequence of events – a funny *story* shown in pictures.

comma: *n* a *punctuation mark*, used to show the natural breaks in a *text(1)*.

commercial: 1. *adj* describing *publishers* and *publications(2)* whose main emphasis is on saleability and profit. 2. *n* a television or radio *advertisement*.

commercial a: *n* the sign @, meaning 'at', used in calculating prices.

commissioned work: *n* a work initiated by a *publisher*, although the idea might be offered by a writer. Having identified a need and demand, or having been convinced by a writer of such a need and demand, the publisher invites the writer to put forward a *proposal* and/or *outline* and *synopsis* to meet the envisaged *concept*. Provided this work is satisfactory, the publisher then gives the writer a *contract*. Established writers might be commissioned without preliminaries.

commissioning editor: see under *editor*.

commonplace book: *n* a book of notes, ideas and *quotations* compiled by an individual; see *eg* W. H. Auden's 'A Certain World' (1971) and John Murray's 'A Gentleman Publisher's Commonplace Book' (1996).

communiqué: *n* an official announcement to the *press* or public.

Compact Disk – Read Only Memory (*abbr* CD-ROM): *n* a high-density storage device.

Compact Disk – Re-Writable (*abbr* CD-RW): *n* a *disk* that can have its contents edited and changed.

company publication: *n* 1. an internal *publication(2)* produced for company employees. 2. an external *publication(2)* produced for a company's clients, shareholders, distributors *etc.*

compendium: *n* a book in which two or more previously published books are put together.

competing work: *n* a work on a topic that is the same as or similar to the subject covered by a contract and which is aimed at largely the same market.

compilation: *n* a work made by putting together material from various sources.

compiler: *n* a person who selects or collects material for a *collection*, a book of quotations, an *anthology etc.*

completion date: *n* the date by which a work must be finished.

complimentary copy: *n* a copy of a book given for no payment. It is standard practice for *publishers* to give *authors* free copies of their books at the time of *publication(1)*, the exact number being specified in the *contract*. Many *small press magazines* pay *contributors* in complimentary copies instead of money.

compose: *v* to set up material ready for reproduction.

compositor: *n* a person who *sets type*.

computer graphics: *pl n* the production of drawings, photographs, *text(1) etc* using computer technology.

conceit: *n* an elaborate *metaphor* or verbal image. (Latin: 'concept'.)

concept: *n* a general idea of a work, its content and *form*.

concertina fold: *n* a method of folding *pamphlets* in which each fold goes in the opposite direction from the one before.

concordance: *n* a *reference book* listing all the different uses of an individual word in an *author's* works or in a particular *text(1)*.

concrete poetry: see *calligramme.*

condensed book: *n* an *abridged* version of a book, usually sold to *book club* subscribers by direct mail.

condensed typeface: *n* a *typeface* with very narrow *characters(2)*.

confession story: *n* a supposedly true-life *story*, almost invariably *fiction*, possibly inspired by real-life problems;

nearly always written in *first person narrative*. 'Sin, suffer, repent' used to be the required formula, but many such stories nowadays take a more tolerant look at problems.

conflict: *n* a struggle or contest between opposing forces: *characters(1)*, beliefs, standards, ethics *etc*.

conjunction: *n* a word that connects sentences, *clauses(2)* and words, *eg* 'and', 'but'.

consistency: *n* agreement throughout a *text(1)* of the various elements of *style*, content and *presentation*; *eg* the use of single or double *quotation marks*, choice of 'ise' or 'ize' *verb* endings, use of *italics*, *bold type*, capitalisation *etc*.

consonance: *n* in *poetry*, the repeated arrangement of consonants with changes of vowels between them, producing a kind of *half-rhyme*; *eg* 'flip-flop', 'ding-dong'. (Latin: 'sounding together'.)

consumable text book: *n* a *text book* designed to be written in by the student, and so usable only once.

consumer magazine: *n* a *publication(2)* covering general affairs, sports, hobbies *etc*, as distinct from business, trade or professional matters.

contemporary romance: *n romantic fiction* set in the present day.

contents/table of contents: *n* a *page*, usually in the *prelims*, which lists *chapter titles*, *subheads* etc., and shows the page numbers on which they begin.

context: *n* the background situation which helps you to understand an event. (Latin: 'woven together'.)

continuation page: *n* a *page* of *text* that follows on from a main page.

continuity: *n* similar to *consistency*; the agreement of elements in a *text(1)*, concerned particularly with names, colours, *settings(2)*, feasibility of actions *etc*. *Eg*, if a *character(1)* is called Sam in the first *chapter* he can't be Simon in a later one unless you give a reason.

contract: *n* an agreement between *publisher* and *author* specifying the responsibilities each party undertakes in the writing, production and marketing of a work, in terms of payment, assignation of *rights*, schedule of writing and publishing *etc*.

contributing editor: see under *editor*.

contribution: *n* a piece of writing supplied to a *publication(2)* or broadcast programme.

contributor: *n* a writer who supplies material for *publication(1)* alongside other writers' work, particularly in a *periodical*.

contributor's copy: *n* a copy of the *issue* of a *publication(2)* in which the *contributor's* work appears. Often the only payment offered by *small presses*. See also *voucher copy*.

cookie: *n* a computer *file* that sends information about a user to the central computer with each request the user makes; the server logs the request and uses the information to send customised data back to the user.

co-operative publishing: *n* a number of people sharing the labour and cost of producing a work, *ie editing, layout*, design, *typesetting*, printing, binding and sales.

co-publishing: *n* an arrangement by which *author* and *publisher* share production costs and (they hope) profits, usually under a contractual *agreement*. Not to be confused with *subsidy publishing* or *vanity publishing*.

copy: *n matter* to be *typeset*. Usually refers to the prepared *typescript*.

copy date: *n* the date by which material is to be delivered to the *editor* or *publisher*. Most *contracts* carry a penalty *clause(1)* covering the writer's obligation to deliver *copy* on time, as delay can cause costly rescheduling of *typesetting*, printing and *promotion*.

copy-editing: *n* preparation of a *typescript* for the printer by a specialist *editor*, either a member of staff or a *freelance*, appointed by the *publisher* to check *facts*, spelling and *punctuation, syntax, continuity, consistency etc*, and possibly to rewrite clumsy or inexact *text(1)*, and to make changes to conform with *house style* where necessary.

copy-editor: see under *editor*.

copy-fitting: *v* 1. working out the typographical *specification* to which a *manuscript* must be *set* to fit into a given space or number of *pages*. See *cast-off*. 2. making *copy* fit a given space by *editing*, and/or by altering the specified *typeface* or *type* size.

copyholder: *n* a *proofreader* who reads aloud to a colleague who checks the *text(1)* word by word, comma by comma, as it is read.

copy preparation (*abbr* **copy prep**): *n* the marking of *copy* with appropriate instructions for the *typesetter*.

copyright: *n* in simple terms, 'the *right* to copy'; the proprietary rights in a work, as defined by law. Copyright in a work is owned by its *author* unless and until it is assigned to someone else. In UK law, copyright exists for the author's lifetime plus 70 years from the end of the year in which he or she dies.

copyright deposit: *n* a requirement in certain countries, including the UK, whereby *publishers* are obliged to deposit with designated libraries a specified number of copies of books and other new *publications(2)* and new *editions*. See *statutory copies*.

copyright fee: *n* a fee paid to a *copyright* holder for *permission* to use their work.

copyright infringement: *n* the illegal copying or use of work that is protected by *copyright*.

copywriting: *v* the writing of material for *advertisements*, *publicity*, *promotions etc*.

coronach: *n* a Scottish and Irish word for a funeral *dirge*. (Gaelic: 'roaring together'.)

correspondence course: *n* a course conducted by postal tuition.

correspondent: *n* a *reporter*, usually a *freelance*, who covers a specified geographical area; also called a *stringer*.

corrigenda: *pl n* a printed list of corrections. (Latin: 'corrections'.)

cost: *v* to estimate the cost of production.

counterplot: *n* a secondary *theme* or *subplot* running concurrently with and in opposition to the main *plot*.

counterpoint: *n* contrast for effect.

couplet: *n* two lines of *verse*, usually rhyming. (Old French: 'little pair'.) See also *heroic couplet*.

course book: *n* a book used by teachers and students as the basis of an educational course.

courtesy line: see *credit*.

cover: *n* the outer section of a *publication(2)*, bearing its *title(1)*.

cover copy: see *blurb*.

cover flat: *n* a sample of a *cover* before it is folded.

cover mount: *n* a free gift attached to the cover of a *magazine*.

cover price: see *list price*.

covering letter: *n* a letter sent to an *agent*, *editor* or *publisher* along with a *proposal* or *manuscript* or other material, giving the writer's contact details and basic information about the enclosure and about the *author* where appropriate, and stating the terms on which the material is offered.

craft: *n* the skill and work involved in turning an idea or *concept* into a publishable item.

craft book: *n* a book dealing with practical work done by hand, *eg* sewing, knitting, painting *etc.*

crc: *abbr* of *camera-ready copy.*

creative writing: *n* generally accepted to mean imaginative rather than factual writing.

creativity: *n* the ability to see things in a new and imaginative way, and so produce something original.

credit: *n* a printed line giving the name of the originator of an *illustration*, diagram, table or *quotation*, and/or the supplier of *artwork*, and/or the individual or organisation who gave *permission* to publish; also called a *courtesy line.*

crime writing: *n fiction* whose subject is crime in any form. See also *true crime writing.*

crisis: *n* a structural element of a *plot*, a crucial or decisive moment involving a turning point in the action. (Greek: 'decision'.)

critic: *n* a professional *reviewer*, skilled in evaluating the qualities of a work.

critical analysis: *n* close investigation of a work, assessing how each of its elements contributes to the work's over-all success or failure.

criticism: *n* analytical evaluation and discussion. (Greek: 'judgment'.)

critique: *n* critical examination and written assessment of a work.

crop: *v* to cut off part(s) of an *illustration.*

crop marks: *n* guidelines indicating which parts of a *page* or *illustration* are not to be included in a reproduction.

crosshead: *n* a centred *heading* for a subsection of a work.

crossover books: *n* books that appeal to both adults and children and which are promoted to both *markets.*

cross-reference: *n* an indication in a book directing the *reader(1)* to information in another part of the book; usually *set* in *italic* (as in this book) or *bold type.*

Crown copyright: *n* the exclusive legal *right* to material produced by government departments – it is illegal to re-produce this without *permission*.

curly bracket: see *brace*.

curiosa: *pl n* books or *texts(1)* dealing with unusual subjects, particularly *erotica*.

current list: *n* a *publisher's list* of *titles* currently available.

curriculum vitae (*abbr* CV): *n* a listing of qualifications and achievements. (Latin: 'programme of life'.)

cursor: *n* a movable marker on a computer screen used to indicate *eg* where *text(1)* should be entered or a correction made.

custom publishing: *n* publishing done specifically to a customer's needs.

cut: *v* to remove part or parts of a *text(1)*. See *cutting(1)*.

cut and paste: *v* a labour-saving device by which *text(1)* can be moved (cut) and placed in a new location (pasted) without retyping. The expression derives from the days when text had to be physically cut out and pasted on paper.

cutback binding: see *perfect binding*.

cutout book: *n* a children's book where the *illustrations* can be cut out and made into models.

cutting: 1. *v* reducing material by cutting or condensing it to fit a given length. 2. *n* an item cut out of a *publication(2)*; also called a *clip* or *clipping*.

cuttings agency: *n* an agency which, for a fee, seeks and cuts out specified references in *newspapers* and magazines and supplies them to a client.

CV: see *curriculum vitae*.

cyberlaw: *n* the law as it relates to computers, *networks* and information systems.

cyberspace: *n* the environment in which electronic information 'exists' or is exchanged.

cybersquatter: *n* someone who registers another person's name on the *Internet*, possibly demanding money for its release.

cycle: *n* a group of *stories*, *novels*, plays or songs all dealing with the same or related subjects, grouped together either by tradition or by the *author*.

cynghanedd: *n* poetic conventions in Welsh *poetry*, involving *internal rhymes* and *alliteration*.

D

dactyl: *n* a metrical *foot* consisting of one stressed *syllable* followed by two unstressed syllables.

dagger: *n* the *symbol(1)* † , a reference mark for *footnotes*.

daily: *n* a *newspaper* published every weekday.

database: *n* systematically organised *files* of information, held on computer and accessible to subscribers.

Data Protection Act: *n* UK legislation passed in 1984 requiring registration by any owner of a *database* that contains personal information about other people.

data transfer rate: *n* the speed at which data is transmitted over a link, measured in *bits per second*.

dateline: *n* a line at the beginning of a *newspaper report* giving the date of the report and the place where it was filed.

dead metaphor: *n* a *metaphor* so over-used it no longer possess any impact; *eg* 'green with envy', 'sick as a parrot'.

deadline: *n* the latest date or time by which a job must be finished.

debug: *v* to find and correct any errors in a computer *program*.

decasyllable: *n* a line of *verse* with ten *syllables*.

dedicated server: *n* a *web server* run by a web hosting provider where a single *website* gets use of the entire computer.

dedication: *n* an expression of an *author's* sentiments towards family and/or friends, usually printed in a book's *prelims*.

defamation: *n* damage in writing to someone's name or reputation; *publication(1)* of defamatory material can be a criminal as well as a civil offence, depending on the circumstances. See also *libel*.

defragment (*abbr* defrag): *v* to organise pieces of *files* on your *hard drive* so that they can be accessed more easily.

déjà-vu: *adj* describing unoriginal material; *eg* a *story* situation that gives a sense of having been read before although it is newly written. (French: 'already seen'.)

delete: *v* to remove a word or a section of *text(1)*.

de luxe edition: *n* an *edition* of higher quality than the regular product, with a more luxurious binding and heavier paper; perhaps given added status as a *limited edition*.

dénouement: *n* the 'winding down' after the *resolution* of a *story*: rounding-off and tying up loose ends. (French: 'unknotting'.)

department: *n* an ongoing section of a *magazine*.

deposit library: *n* a library to which, by law, a *publisher* must give a copy of every book he publishes. See *statutory deposit copy*.

descender: *n* the part of a *lower case* letter that descends below the depth of the letter x, *eg* p, q. See also *ascender*.

desk editor: see under *editor*.

desktop: *n* the computer screen, where *icons* for *programs*, *files* and equipment are shown.

desktop publishing (*abbr* DTP): *n* publishing by computer *programs* which let you design *pages* on screen instead of pasting them up on paper.

detached autobiography: *n* a device in *fiction* by which events are recalled after enough time has passed for the *narrator* to look at them from a more mature and analytical *viewpoint* than that held when they happened; see *eg* Daphne du Maurier's *novel* 'Rebecca' (1938).

detached viewpoint: *n* a *viewpoint* in which the *reader(1)* is shown action and given description as the story unfolds, but without *exposition*, interpretation or perception by any *character(1)*.

detective fiction: *n crime fiction* in which a detective plays the main *role*.

deus ex machina: *n* a device by which the *characters'(1)* problems are resolved by someone or something not previously mentioned. Originally, in Greek theatre, a character not seen, heard or mentioned until he arrives on the stage at the end of the play to explain and sort out all the problems. (Latin: 'god out of a machine'.)

Dewey Decimal Classification System: *n* a system used in most UK libraries to classify the main book subjects into easy-to-locate categories:

000 General Works
100 Philosophy
200 Religion
300 Social Sciences
400 Languages
500 Science

600 Technology
700 Arts and Recreations
800 Literature
900 Biography, History and Geography

diaeresis: *n* two dots placed above the second of two vowels to show that each should be pronounced separately; *eg* 'naïve'.

dialect: *n* the distinctive language of a particular social class, ethnic group or geographical region. (Greek: 'language of a district'.)

dialectic: *n* the investigation of truth by discussion. (Greek: 'art of discourse'.)

dialogue: *n* conversation between two or more people. To ensure clarity in a *manuscript*, each speaker should be given a new line of *text(1)*; their speech should not be started in a *paragraph* containing a previous speaker's words. (Greek: 'conversation'.)

diary: *n* 1. a regular record of events in a person's life, perhaps with thoughts and feelings about those events. 2. a regular news or *gossip column(2)* in a *newspaper*. (Latin: 'daily'.)

diary narration: *n* a story told in the form of *diary(1)* entries.

digest: *n* 1. a *synopsis* of a work, conveying a sense of the main substance of that work. 2. a *magazine* containing condensed versions of books or *articles* which have been published elsewhere.

digital rights: *n* the *right* to publish in digital form.

digital video disk (*abbr* DVD): *n* an optical compact *disk* for storing video, audio or other information.

digital video disk read only memory (*abbr* DVD-ROM): *n* a high capacity optical disk on which data can be stored but not over-written.

digizine: *n* a *magazine* in digital form, either on the *Internet* or on *disk*.

dilemma: *n* a problem where a *character(1)* must choose between alternative courses, neither of which he really wants to take.

dime novel: *n* a cheap *paperback novel*.

dingbat: *n* a small decorative element in *typesetting*.

diphthong: *n* two vowel-sounds pronounced as one *syllable* and printed as one *character(2)*, as in *eg* 'æ'.

direct speech: *n characters'(1)* words set out exactly as they would be said; usually indicated by enclosing the spoken words in *quotation marks*. See also *indirect speech*.

dirge: *n* a funeral song or hymn.

dirty copy: *n copy* with many corrections and amendments.

dirty proof: *n* a *proof* showing many errors, or one marked heavily with corrections and amendments.

disappearing hero: *n* a term used by *editors* of *romantic fiction* to describe over-concentration on the *heroine* – her appearance, feelings, activities *etc* – to the near-exclusion of the *hero*, resulting in an unbalanced, unsatisfactory and unconvincing relationship between the principal *characters(1)*.

disclaimer: *n* a legal refusal to accept responsibility; a 'get-out' *clause(1)*.

disk: *n* a flat round cassette for recording computer information.

disk operating system (*abbr* **DOS**): *n* the part of a computer operating system that controls *disk* and *file* management.

display matter: *n titles(1)*, headings *etc* set in larger and sometimes more ornate *typefaces* than those used in the *text(1)*.

dissonance: *n* words and *rhythms* that grate on the ear. (Latin: 'disagreement in sound'.) *Eg*, from Robert Browning's 'Childe Roland to the Dark Tower Came' (1855):

> What made those holes and rents
> In the dock's harsh swarth leaves, bruised as to baulk
> All hope of greenness . . .'

document: *n* a *file* containing information such as *text(1)*, *graphics* or sound. (Latin: 'official paper'.)

doggerel: *n* rough clumsy *verse*; *eg*

> 'So let the beautiful city of Glasgow flourish
> And may the inhabitants always find food their
>   bodies to nourish . . .'
> (William Topaz McGonagall, 1830–1902.)

domain: *n* an area of the *Internet* owned or shared by users.

domain name: *n* the part of an *e-mail* address that follows the @ *symbol(1)*, identifying a particular *Internet site*.

dongle: *n* a small plug-in tool that enables a computer to read protected *software*.

donnée: *n* a fact or facts 'given' to the *reader(1)*, from which other information might be inferred; *eg* a given situation which conditions the reader to make basic assumptions about a *character(1)* or a story. 2. the origin (idea, word, phrase, experience) of a work. (French: 'given'.)

DOS: see *disk operating system*.

double dagger: *n* the *symbol(1)* ‡ used as a reference mark for a *footnote*.

double entendre: *n* an ambiguity; used almost exclusively to imply a *pun* with a sexual connotation. (French: 'hearing twice'.)

double page spread: see *double spread*.

double quotation marks: *n* printed signs " " used to show that a piece of *text(1)* has been quoted.

double spacing/double line spacing: *n* one full line, the depth of a typed line, left blank between lines of *type*; does <u>not</u> mean two spaces between words.

double spread/double page spread: *n* a single *illustration* running across two facing *pages* with no other illustration on those pages. See also *centre fold*.

download: *v* to transfer data or *programs* from one computer to another.

draft: *n* a preliminary version of *copy* or of an *illustration*.

drama: *n* a work which is only completely conveyed in performance, although it might be published in print. (Greek: 'action'.)

dramatic irony: *n* a situation or utterance whose significance is not perceived at the time; occurs, *eg*, in a play when the audience knows more than the *characters(1)* and can foresee the oncoming *tragedy* or *comedy*.

drop-down menu: *n* a list of options that appears below a heading when it is clicked on a computer screen.

DTP: see *desktop publishing*.

dummy: *n* a mock-up of a proposed *publication(2)* in the correct *format* using the correct paper but without the complete *text(1)*. Might contain sample *pages* showing *type* and *illustrations*, or a repeated *signature* of printed pages.

dust jacket/dust wrapper: *n* a loose, heavy paper cover on a *hardback* book; usually illustrated, it bears the book's *title*, the *author's* name, probably a *blurb*, and perhaps some biographical comments and/or *puffs*.

dust wrapper: see *dust jacket*.

DVD: see *digital video disk*.

DVD-ROM: see *digital video disk read only memory*.

dystopia: *n* an unpleasant imaginary world; the opposite of *Utopia*; see Aldous Huxley's 'Brave New World' (1932). (Greek: 'bad place'.)

E

earned out: *n* a term applied when a book's earned *royalties* have reached the amount of the *advance* paid to its *author*.

e-book: see *electronic book*

e-book reader: *n* a hand-held computer screen for downloading and reading *e-books*.

eclectic: *adj* wide-ranging in taste. (Greek: 'chosen'.)

edit: *v* to check, correct, arrange and prepare *copy*. (Latin: 'produce'.)

edition: *n* one printing of a book. A second or subsequent edition will have alterations, sometimes substantial.

editor: *n* a catch-all title for anyone working on material to be published. Various editors are responsible for processes ranging from selecting *manuscripts* to seeing work into print. The usual (but not invariable) functions are:

acquisitions/acquiring editor: *n* one who finds and buys new book *manuscripts* for their company.

assistant editor: *n* a deputy who can stand in for an editor in their absence.

commissioning editor: *n* a person who engages an *author* or artist to supply work.

contributing editor: *n* an expert on a subject of particular interest to a *magazine's readership*, who *vets* material on that subject and/or contributes regularly, but who is not on the magazine's staff.

copy-editor: *n* a person who corrects and alters *copy* to bring it up to the *publisher's* standard and *style*, to ensure *consistency*, *continuity* and accuracy of spelling, *punctuation*, grammar, *syntax etc*.

desk editor: *n* a person who takes close control of a work from receipt of the *manuscript* to the finished book;

so-called simply because most of the work is done at a desk which is the hub of the relevant functions.

editor: *n* a title given to a person in charge of a *magazine* or of a specific project or area of publishing within a *house*.

features editor: *n* a person who buys or commissions *features* for a *newspaper* or *magazine*.

fiction editor: *n* a person who buys or commissions *fiction* for a *magazine* or *publishing house*.

house editor: *n* same as *copy-editor*.

initiating editor: *n* an editor who initiates new projects which are then passed on for other editors to carry through.

line editor: *n* same as *copy-editor*.

managing editor: *n* a person who supervises editors who are less senior, or possibly an editor who also manages the company.

picture editor: *n* a person who is responsible for locating and acquiring illustrative material.

sub-editor: *n* a person whose duties are similar to those of a *copy-editor* but who has more authority and responsibility. Duties usually cover correcting grammar and *syntax*, making any changes necessary to improve *readability*, checking any doubtful *facts* or allegations, dividing *text(1)* into sub-sections where appropriate, altering *type* sizes where necessary. Each *publisher* has his or her own policy on sub-editing. 'Sub-editor' is a title in its own right; it does not mean a deputy editor.

editorial: *n* 1. a *publication(2)*'s formal views, opinions and comments on a particular topic, set in a special *column(2)* usually written by the *editor*, or by a guest *contributor* who might be a specialist on that topic, or a 'famous name' writer. Nowadays usually called a *leader(1)*. 2. in *magazine* and *newspaper* publishing today refers to *text(1)* that is not *advertising copy*.

editorial assistant: *n* usually the first step in a publishing career. One who works closely with an *editor*, doing the more routine jobs involved in the various editing processes.

editorial calendar: *n* a detailed schedule of a *publication(2)*'s future content.

editorial policy: *n* an *editor*'s over-all concept of the kind of *publication(2)* he or she wants to produce. Editors might have a free hand in this, or they might have to follow specific guidelines and policies set out by the *publisher*.

editorial requirements: *n* specification of the kind of material an *editor* wants from *contributors*.

educational publisher: *n* a *publisher* of books for use in schools and colleges.

edutainment: *n media* intended both to educate and to entertain.

EFL: *abbr* of 'English as a foreign language'.

eg: *n abbr* of the Latin 'exempli gratia', meaning 'for example'.

eiron: *n* a stock *character(1)* from Greek *comedy*, a modest individual who contrasts with the *alazon*. (Greek: 'irony'.)

electronic book: *n* a book stored on computer *file* to be read on screen rather than printed out on paper.

electronic rights: *n* the *right* to publish electronically.

electronic publishing: *n* publishing in electronic form (on computer, on *disk*, *online etc*), not on paper.

electronic submission: *n* a *submission* made by *e-mail* or on a computer *disk*.

electronic typescript: *n typescript* in electronic form on computer or *disk*.

elegy: *n* a poetic lament for the dead. See *eg* 'Elegy Written in a Country Churchyard' by Thomas Gray (1751).

elephant folio: *n* the largest size of *folio*, about sixty centimetres tall.

elision: *n* the omission of something considered inessential; *eg* in *poetry* 'the' might be shortened to 'th' for ease of pronunciation, as in 'th' Eternal spring'; or in numbers, '54–55' becoming '54–5' or '256–267' becoming '256–67'. (Latin: 'crush out'.)

ellipsis: *n* a sequence of dots . . . , indicating an omission. (Latin: 'leaving out'.)

ELT: see *English Language Teaching*.

em: *n* a unit of measurement equal to the width of the letter 'm' in any *typeface*.

e-mail: *n* electronic mail, sent via the *Internet*.

EML: see *Extensible Markup Language*.

emoticon: *n* a facial expression made up of *characters(2)* to convey an emotion, *eg* :-) for a smile or joke (also called a 'smiley'), :-(for sadness or dislike.

emotional drive: *n* the motivating force that drives a

character(1): love, hate, greed, jealousy, ambition, vengeance *etc.*

en: *n* a unit of measurement half the width of an *em*.

encryption: *n* the conversion of plain *text(1)* to a secure coded form by means of a cipher system.

encyclopaedia: *n* a book or a set of books offering information on general or specified areas of knowledge. (Greek: 'general education'.)

end pages: *n* the pages of a book that follow the main *text(1)*.

end matter: see *back matter*.

end notes: *n* notes placed at the end of the relevant *chapter* or at the end of a book instead of being placed at the *foot(1)* of the relevant *page*.

endorsement: *n* a quote from a well-known person or a specialist in a book's field, printed on the cover and/or on marketing material to promote sales. See also *puff*.

endpapers: *n* strong paper *leaves* which are stuck down to the inner sides of the back and front *boards* to secure a book to its *case*.

end-rhyme: *n* the most common form of *rhyme*, with *syllables* rhyming at the end of lines of *verse*.

end-stopped line: *n* a line of *poetry* that has a natural pause at the end.

English cosy: see *teacake novel*.

English Language Teaching (abbr *ELT*): *n* the teaching of the English language to non-native students, a sector of educational publishing.

English sonnet: *n* another name for *Shakespearian sonnet*. See *sonnet*.

enhanced e-book: *n* an *e-book* which incorporates additional effects like video and sound.

enjambment: *n* the opposite of *end-stopped*; means that lines of *poetry* run on coherently from each other. (French: 'striding'.) *Eg*, from William Wordsworth's 'There was a Boy' (1800):

> And, when there came a pause
> Of silence such as baffled his best skill:
> Then sometimes, in that silence, while he hung
> Listening, a gentle shock of mild surprise
> Has carried far into his heart the voice
> Of mountain torrents . . .

envelopes and folders are labelled in 'C' sizes as follows:

C0	917 mm x 1297 mm
C1	648 mm x 917 mm
C2	458 mm x 648 mm
C3	324 mm x 458 mm
C4	229 mm x 324 mm
C5	162 mm x 229 mm
C6	114 mm x 162 mm
C7	81 mm x 114 mm
C7/6	81 mm x 162 mm
DL	110 mm x 220 mm

ephemera: *pl n* printed material such as programmes, labels, tickets, *pamphlets*, bookmarks, calendars, postcards *etc.* (Greek: 'living a day'.)

epic: *n* a very long *narrative poem* about a heroic person or event, *eg* the 'Iliad' and 'Odyssey' (8th century BC, traditionally attributed to Homer), and Milton's 'Paradise Lost' (1667 and 1674).

epigram: *n* a very short witty *poem* or saying. (Greek: 'inscription'.) *Eg*

You beat your pate, and fancy wit will come;
Knock as you please, there's nobody at home!
(Alexander Pope, 1688–1744.)

epigraph: *n* a *quotation* in a book's *prelims* or at the beginning of a *part* or *chapter*. (Greek: 'written upon'.)

epilogue: *n* the concluding part of a work. (Greek: 'speech on'.)

episode: *n* 1. an incident or occurrence. 2. a part of a radio or television *serial.* (Greek: 'coming in besides'.)

epistolary: *adj* in the form of correspondence. (Greek: 'to send on the occasion'.) See *letter narration.*

epitaph: *n* words engraved on a person's tombstone, commenting on their life. (Greek: 'upon a tomb'.)

epithet: *n* an *adjective* or adjectival phrase defining a special quality or attribute; *eg* 'heather-covered hills'. (Greek: 'something added'.)

epitome: *n* 1. an *abridgment* of a longer work. 2. a typical example. (Greek: 'cut short'.)

epyllion: *n* a short, narrative *poem.* (Greek: 'little poem'.)

erotica: *pl n* sexually oriented adult *fiction*.

erratum (*pl* errata) slip: *n* a last-minute correction after a book has been printed; usually takes the form of a *tip-in* but is sometimes inserted loose between two *pages* of the *prelims*.

escalator clause: *n* a *clause(1)* in a *contract* allowing for the *author* of a book to receive an increased *royalty* after a specified number of copies has been sold.

esoteric: *adj* describes literature intended for *readers(1)* with a specialised knowledge of or interest in a particular subject.

essay: *n* a *prose* composition which discusses a subject or expresses a point of view in non-technical terms. A formal essay is relatively impersonal, knowledgeable, considered, but not pretentious. An informal essay is more relaxed, intimate and personal, usually deals with a lighter topic, and is often spiced with *humour* and *anecdote*. (Latin: 'to weigh'.)

essayist: *n* a person who writes *essays*.

estimate: *n* an estimated calculation of the cost of producing a book. (An estimate of *extent* is called a *cast-off*.)

etc: see *et cetera*.

et cetera (*abbr etc*): Latin for 'and the rest', 'and so on'.

et seq: see *et sequens*.

et sequens (*abbr et seq*): Latin for 'and following'.

euphemism: *n* a hard fact stated in soft terms; *eg* 'Mother has gone to a better place' instead of 'Mother has died'. (Greek: 'speaking fair'.)

euphony: *n* language which is smooth and pleasing to the ear. (Greek: 'well-sounding'.)

even pages: *n* the *pages* of a book with even numbers, usually the left-hand pages.

even small caps: *n small capitals* with no full *capitals*.

evergreen: *n* a timeless *article* whose subject matter doesn't date.

excerpt: *n* a passage selected from a work for *quotation* or for reading, or as a subject for evaluation and/or *criticism*.

excise: *v* to cut something out.

exclamation mark: *n* a mark ! used for emphasis or to express astonishment; known as 'screamers' in the publishing business and often over-used by novice writers.

exclusivity: *n* the exclusive *right* to *market(2)* a product in a specific area.

exhibitionism: *n* inclusion of *facts* or theories that contribute nothing, simply to show off knowledge or *research*.

explication: *n* the detailed *analysis* of a piece of writing, revealing its merits and its flaws. (Latin: 'unfolding'.)

explicit description: *n* clear and detailed description, usually of sexual or violent activities.

exposé: *n journalism* that reveals 'secrets', real or imagined, about a person, event or situation, usually to someone's discredit.

exposition: *n* explanation of and/or commentary on events, actions, *characters'(1)* feelings and the like; 'telling' rather than 'showing'.

expurgate: *v* to remove material which might offend a general *readership*. (Latin: 'purify out'.)

Extensible Markup Language (*abbr* EML): *n* a means of making *web documents* self-describing so that they can be formatted with *database*-style fields. Also *XML*.

extent: *n* the length of a book stated in *pages*.

extract: *n* material quoted from another source, usually *set* in a different size of *type* and/or indented.

eyeballs: *n* slang for the number of visits made to a *website*.

eye rhymes: *n* rhymed words with similar spellings but different pronunciation; *eg* 'home/come', 'flow/now'.

e-zine: *n* a *magazine* created, distributed and read on-screen.

F

fable: *n* a story that instructs and/or amuses, illustrating a principle of human behaviour or making a moral point; *eg* Aesop's tales from the 6th century BC. (Latin: 'discourse'.)

fabliau: *n* a medieval form; a short satiric or comic tale told in *verse*, *eg* Chaucer's 'The Miller's Tale' (late 14th century).

facing pages: *n* the two visible *pages* of an open book.

facsimile (*abbr* fax): *n* an exact reproduction. (Latin: 'to make alike'.) See *fax machine*.

facsimile edition: *n* an exact copy of a previously published work, generally of specialist or antiquarian interest; usually produced by using a copy of the original work as *camera ready copy*.

fact: *n* a reality, something that exists or happens, or has existed or happened, as distinct from an idea or belief.

fact checker: *n* a person who checks factual information in *articles* and books on behalf of a *publisher*, to ensure accuracy; might be an employee or a *freelance*.

faction: *n* writing which blurs the distinction between *fact* and *fiction*, without regard to what is true and real and what is not.

fair comment: *n* the expression of an honestly held opinion, given in good faith; sometimes used as a defence against an accusation of *libel*.

fair copy: *n* a correction-free copy of a *document* or *manuscript*.

fair dealing: *n* the use of *copyright* material for purposes of private study, *criticism* or *review*. Not defined in law, the term is open to interpretation, but is generally accepted as meaning that you can quote a line or two to illustrate a point, provided you make due acknowledgement of the source of the *quotation*; also called 'fair use' in the USA. The rules on fair dealing vary from country to country. Check the laws of the country in which you live/work.

fair use: see *fair dealing*.

fairy tale: *n* a *genre* of children's *fiction* based on magic and on imaginary beings such as fairies, gnomes, witches *etc*.

false plant: same as *red herring*.

false scent: same as *red herring*.

family saga: *n* a *novel* spanning many years and, usually, several generations of the same family.

fantasy: *n* any *story* not based on realistic *characters(1)* or *settings(2)* but on highly imaginative happenings. (Greek: 'imagination'.)

fanzine: *n* a magazine, usually promoting a popular music group or artist, sometimes officially produced by the group or artist's fan club, sometimes unofficially by fans.

FAQ(s): see *frequently asked question(s)*.

farce: *n* a *comedy* of action, *eg* Brandon Thomas's 'Charley's Aunt' (1892). (Latin: 'to stuff'.)

farm out: *v* to hand work out to another person or company.

favicon: *n* a favourite *icon*.

fax: see *facsimile*.

fax machine: *n* a machine which scans *documents*, photographs *etc* electronically and transfers them by telephone line to a receiving machine which reproduces and prints out the transmitted material.

FBSR: see *First British Serial Rights*.

feature: *n* a *magazine* or *newspaper article* that is not one of a series. Usually refers to a *human interest piece* as distinct from a news item. See also *short feature*.

feature writer: *n* a *journalist* who writes *features* as distinct from news reports.

features editor: see under *editor*.

feet: *pl* of *foot(2)*.

feminist press: *n* a *publisher* mainly if not exclusively concerned with women's lives – their rights, social and economic conditions *etc*.

festschrift: *n* writings by various people collected in honour of, *eg*, a writer or scholar. (German: 'celebration writing'.)

fiction: *n* writing that is not and does not pretend to be truth but is entirely drawn from the imagination. Sometimes based on *fact* but not claiming to be factual. (Latin: 'fashioned'.)

fictitious: *adj* not true or existing.

fieldwork: *n* the gathering of information by direct investigation rather than reading.

figure: *n* an *illustration*, usually a drawing, table or graph, referred to in a *text(1)*.

figure of speech: *n* any device that uses words to make a striking effect. See, *eg*, *metaphor*.

file: *n* a collection of information.

file attachment: *n* a *file* attached to a message sent by *e-mail*.

file copy: *n* 1. a copy of a book or *magazine* kept for reference. 2. a copy of a book in which corrections, alterations and *updates* are noted.

file transfer protocol (*abbr* FTP): *n* the means of *uploading files* for electronic transfer.

filler: *n* a short item or *illustration* filling a space which would otherwise be blank: *humour*, *anecdotes*, odd *facts*, *light verse*, *quotations*, puzzles, jokes, *cartoons etc*.

film rights: *n* the *right* to make a film based on a published work.

film script: *n* the *text(1)* of a film, with *dialogue* and directing instructions.

find and replace: see *search and replace*.

fine rule: *n* a very thin line.

fine tune: *v* to make small, sometimes subtle and delicate, adjustments to a *text(1)* to bring it up to the required standard.

firewall: *n* computer *software* which prevents unauthorised access to *files* or data.

First British Serial Rights (*abbr* **FBSR**): the *right* to publish an *article* or *story* for the first time and once only in the UK. (Not used with reference to books.)

first draft: *n* the first complete version of a work.

first edition: *n* a book from the first batch of copies printed.

first person narrative: *n* a *story* told in the first person, *ie* from the *viewpoint* of a *narrator* using the personal 'I' rather than the impersonal 'he' or 'she'. The narrator could be any *character(1)*, but is usually the main character.

first proof: *n* the earliest *proof* of a work, checked by the *typesetter* or by the *publisher's proofreader*.

first refusal: see *option clause*.

five senses: *n* essential to successful *romantic fiction*, these are touch, smell, sight, taste and hearing.

fixed costs: *n* production costs which don't alter, no matter how many copies are printed: *typesetting*, designers' fees *etc*. See *unit cost*.

flag: *n* 1. a banner-line on the front cover of a *publication(2)* drawing attention to an item within. See also *masthead*. 2. a mark attached to information on a computer enabling that information to be found again easily.

flame: *v* to rage at someone online.

flap: *n* the part of a *jacket* that folds inside a book's cover.

flash: *n* a *plug-in* which allows *browsers* to display animation.

flashback: *n* a device by which information is given about events that took place before the action of a *story* began, by going back in time to show the *reader(1)* those events as they happened, instead of simply narrating them.

flash drive: *n* a flash memory data storage device integrated with a *USB* interface.

flash fiction: *n* very short *fiction*, usually less than 500 words.

flashforward: *n* a literary device similar to a *flashback*, but depicting events in the future.

flat fee: *n* a negotiated set fee paid to an *author*, *illustrator* or *freelance* for a specific piece of work. No further payments are made, nor are there any *royalties*.

flat rate: *n* a fixed charge or payment which is the same for everyone.

flier: *n* a small *advertising* leaflet.

flop: *n* a reversed image, either deliberate or accidental.

flush left/right: *adj* describing *text(1)* that is aligned at left/right.

flyleaf: *n* an *endpaper* in a book.

focus: *n* in writing, sharp clear definition of and concentration on the subject, without wandering off it or introducing irrelevancies.

foil: *n* a contrasting *character(1)* or event or item that brings out the qualities or characteristics of another.

folder: *n* an area for storing *files* to keep them organised.

fold-out: *n* a large *page* folded to fit into a book, designed to be unfolded for reading; mainly used for maps, diagrams *etc*.

folio: *n* 1. a *leaf*. 2. a *page* number. 3. a *manuscript* page. (Latin: 'leaf'.)

folklore: *n* a collective name for *legends*, superstitions, *stories*, songs *etc*, handed down through generations, usually by word of mouth.

follow copy: *v* an instruction to *typesetter* and *proofreader* to *set* and not to alter what is written, however unorthodox or inconsistent and/or misspelled it appears to be.

follow on: see *run on*.

font (also fount): *n* a specific design of *type*.

foot: *n* 1. the bottom of a *page*. 2. in *poetry*, a unit within a line of *verse*, plural *feet*.

foot margin: *n*; the *margin* at the bottom of a *page*.

footer: *n* running *page* numbers or other *matter* at the *foot(1)* of pages.

footnote: *n* an explanatory note printed at the *foot(1)* of a *page* or below a table, usually identified by a *symbol(1)*, *eg* an *asterisk*, with a corresponding symbol in the *text(1)* or in the body of the table.

fore-edge: *n* the outer edge of a *page*.

foreign rights/foreign language rights: *n subsidiary rights* granting *permission* for a work to be published in a foreign country and/or in a foreign language.

foreshadow: *v* to mention something often and/or pointedly enough to implant its significance in the *reader(1)'s* mind, preparing them for an event or events to come.

foreword: *n* an *introduction* to a work or to its *author*, sometimes written by an expert in the book's subject, or possibly by a well-known 'name', to lend authority to the work.

form: *n* the structural unity of a work, its arrangement and *style*. (Latin: 'shape'.)

format: 1. *n* size, shape and general *layout*. 2. *v* to prepare a *disk* for having *files* written on to it.

formula novel: *n* a *novel* written to a 'recipe' in accordance with a *publisher's guidelines*, with a specified *story structure* and standard *characters(1)* and written to a prescribed length.

foul copy: *n copy* with many errors.

'found' poetry: *n* a passage of *prose* 'discovered' and considered 'poetic' enough to be set out in lines like *poetry*.

fount: see *font*.

fourth estate: *n newspapers* and *magazines*, regarded as the fourth political power in the land after the lords temporal (peers), the lords spiritual (bishops) and the commons.

frame: *n* the skeleton *plot* and *structure* on which a *story* is built.

frame within a frame: see *story within a story*.

framing device: *n* a *narrative* device where the opening and closing *scenes* in a *story* occur in a different time from that in which the main action happens.

freebie: *n slang* for a *publication(2)* distributed free of charge to householders, airline and rail travellers *etc*. Usually supported only by *advertising* revenue, many do not pay *freelance contributors*.

freelance (also freelancer): *n* a self-employed person who sells his or her services or written work to a *publisher* for an agreed fee, *ie*, a writer or *journalist* selling work to various *publications(2)* but not employed by any one publisher. Derives from the mercenary knights and soldiers who wandered Europe after the Crusades, hiring out their services as lancers.

free sheet: *n* a *newspaper* that is given away free.

free verse: *n verse* that disregards the conventions of *rhyme*, *metre*, line length *etc*.

freeware: *n software* that is in the *public domain* and can be freely used by anyone.

free writing: *v* writing about whatever comes to mind,

without planning or conscious thought. Pouring out words as they occur, not with a view to *publication(1)* but simply to let the mind wander freely. Practised and highly valued by many writers who recommend it as a cure for *writer's block*.

frequently asked questions (*abbr* FAQs): *n* the questions that come up most often in any subject.

frontispiece: *n* an *illustration* facing the *title page*.

front list: *n* a *publisher's list* of books new to the current season.

front matter: *n* the same as *prelims*.

FTP: see *file transfer protocol*.

full out: *adj* not indented.

full rhyme: *n rhyme* in which the final sounds of the words are the same, *eg* 'moon/June', 'rain/lane'.

full page: *n* one whole *page*.

function key: *n* a computer key which activates a particular set of instructions.

futuristic romance: *n* a *subgenre* of *romantic fiction* in which stories are set in the future.

G

galley proof: *n* the first *proof* taken after the *text(1)* has been *typeset* and before it is made up into *pages*. So-called because in traditional letterpress printing *type* is held in long metal trays called galleys.

game book: *n* a book requiring the *reader(1)'s* active participation.

garbage in, garbage out (*abbr* GIGO): a computing term meaning that the quality of the information put in determines the quality of the information that can be got out.

gatefold: *n* the same as *foldout*.

gay press/gay literature: *n publishers* and *publications(2)* concerned, usually exclusively, with the interests of lesbians and homosexual men.

gazetteer: *n* an *index* of geographical place names, often included for clarification in *eg* travel *guides*.

general books: *n* books which a *publisher* considers too important to be categorised into *genres*, or which don't fit into any recognisable category.

general interest article: *n* an *article* with a broad *reader(1)* appeal, that doesn't fit any specific category.

general interest magazine: *n* a *magazine* of no specific category, but appealing to a broad *readership*.

genre: *n* a species or category of literature. (French: 'type'.)

genre fiction: *n* popular *fiction*; *eg romance, thriller, detective, fantasy etc.*

ghosting/ghost-writing: *n* the *craft* of the *ghost-writer*.

ghost-writer: *n* one who writes in conjunction with someone else (often a celebrity but could be anyone with a saleable story) as if the work had been written by that person; it is unusual for any *credit* to be given to the writer, but occasionally a writer who specialises in and is recognised for this type of work is credited along with the named writer, *eg* 'with Andrew Crofts'.

GIF: see *graphics interchange format.*

gift book: *n* a book designed for the gift *market(1)*. Often in a small *format* and written to fit a particular niche (for mothers, fathers, grandfathers, cat- and dog-lovers, golfers *etc*) and displayed near tills and check-outs to tempt the impulse buyer.

GIGO: *abbr* of *garbage in, garbage out.*

glamour: *n* a category of *magazine* devoted to feminine beauty.

gloss: *n* an explanation of a difficult word or phrase, either in the *margins* or in a note. (Greek: 'foreign language'.)

glossary: *n* an alphabetical list of words or terms related to a subject, with definitions.

glossy: *n* a highly illustrated *magazine* printed on thick glossy paper.

gobbledegook: *n* a word signifying nonsense, usually referring to the over-use of professional *jargon.*

golden rectangle: see *golden section.*

golden section/golden rectangle: *n* ideal proportions for a *page* and a *type* area, based on the ratio 34:21.

gossip column: *n* a *column(2)* made up of short pieces of gossipy news or rumour.

gothic: 1. *n* a heavy black square-cut *typeface*, also called *black letter*. 2. *adj* describing stories of *mystery* and *horror*; originally applied to 18th-century *novels* full of gloom and doom, set against sinister and mysterious *backgrounds*, *eg* Mervyn Peake's 'Gormenghast' *trilogy.*

gothic romance: *n* a *subgenre* of *romantic fiction*, describing *stories* full of dark menace and almost invariably featuring a woman in jeopardy.

grammage: *n* the metric measure of paper expressed in grams per square metre. See *gsm*.

graphic novel: *n* a *novel* published in the form of a *comic strip*.

graphics: *n* drawings, diagrams and pictures in printed or animated work.

graphics interchange format (GIF): *n* one of the two most used graphics *formats* on the *web*. See also JPEG.

greek: *n* a mix of meaningless letters used to imitate *text(1)* in a *layout*.

green writing: *n* writing concerned with environmental issues.

greengrocer's plural: *n* a term of mild derision applied to the placing of an *apostrophe* before the letter 's' in a plural noun so that it reads as a possessive; so-called because of its extensive use in advertising on market stalls and the like, *eg* 'apple's', 'potato's'.

grids: *n* guidelines used in design.

grout: *n slang* for *filler*.

gsm: *n abbr* of grams per square metre: the specification of weight for paper; also called grammage.

guide: *n* a guidebook giving information about a particular geographical area or about a particular subject.

guidelines/writers' guidelines: *n* specification of *editors'* or *publishers'* requirements, detailing the kind of material they want, like subject matter, length, *style etc.*

guillotine: *n* a device for cutting paper and card.

gumshoe: *n slang* for *private detective*; often used in *pulp fiction*.

gutter: *n* the inside *margin* between two facing *pages* of *type*.

gutter press: *n* a general description of sensational *journalism*. Applied to *newspapers* and other *publications(2)* that 'dig the dirt' on people and publish to the limit of what is legal and decent (and sometimes beyond). Also called 'yellow press'.

H

hache (US 'hash'): *n* the symbol #, used to indicate the word 'number' or, in proofreading and *text(1)* correction, to indicate a space.

hack: 1. *n* a derogatory term for someone who writes primarily for money. 2. *v* to make unauthorised access into computer networks.

hackneyed writing: *n* humdrum, over-used and unimaginative words, phrases and *plots*. See also *cliché*.

hagiography: *n* literature concerning the lives of the Christian saints. (Greek: 'holy writing'.)

haiku: *n* a Japanese *verse* form of seventeen *syllables* in three lines of five, seven and five syllables; *eg*

> The small tongue of fire
> licks the dry twig, likes the taste,
> consumes the forest.

half-rhyme: *n* an *imperfect rhyme*.

half-title: *n* 1. the *title(1)* of a book as printed on the *recto page* that precedes the *title page*. 2. the page on which the half-title is printed. Also called 'bastard title'.

half-title verso: *n* the left-hand *page* backing the *half-title*. Sometimes blank, but might list the *author's* previous works and/or other authors' works in the same series or on related topics.

half-tone: *n* patterns of black dots which photographically reproduce an *illustration* that requires varying depths of tone.

handbook: *n* a practical *manual* on a specific subject.

handout: *n* 1. a *press release*. 2. a printed leaflet giving supporting information about a lecture or talk.

hanging indent: *n* the first line of a *paragraph set* flush to the left-hand *margin*, with subsequent lines indented a uniform *measure*. Also called *reverse indent*.

harangue: *n* an impassioned speech designed to arouse action.

hardback: *n* a book bound in boards rather than paper or card.

hard-boiled fiction: *n detective fiction*, usually American, with a tough, cynical *style* and *tone*; *eg* Mickey Spillane's 'Mike Hammer' *novels*.

hard copy: *n copy* printed on paper, as distinct from copy stored electronically on *disk* or computer memory.

hard drive: *n* a magnetic *disk*, usually built into a computer, capable of holding much more data than a removable one.

hard sell: *n* forceful selling tactics, *eg* making persistent phone calls or visits.

hb: *abbr* of *hardback*.

head: *n* 1. the top of a *page*. 2. *abbr* of *headline*. 3. *abbr* of *head margin*.

head margin: *n* the *margin* at the top of a *page*.

header: *n* a *running headline*.

heading: *n* a word, phrase, *title* or name at the beginning of a *chapter* or part.

headline: *n* a *displayed* line or lines at the top of a *page* or piece of *text(1)*.

headword: *n* the main entry word in a dictionary.

heavy: *n* a 'quality' *newspaper* like 'The Times', 'The Telegraph'.

heptameter: *n* a line of seven *feet* in English *poetry*.

Her Majesty's Stationery Office (*abbr* HMSO): the *publications(2)* office of the British Government.

hero: *n* the principal male *character(1)*. See also *anti-hero*.

heroic couplet: *n* the most common form of *rhyming couplet*, written in *iambic pentameters*. *Eg* the opening couplet of Alexander Pope's 'Epistle II: To A Lady (Of the Characters of Women)' (1735):

> Nothing so true as what you once let fall,
> 'Most women have no characters at all.'

heroine: *n* the principal female *character(1)*. See also *anti-heroine*.

hexameter: *n* a metrical line of six *feet*.

highlight: *v* to select an item for further action; highlighting is shown by the word or section selected being displayed or marked in a different colour.

historical fiction: *n fiction* in which stories and *characters(1)* might be set against historically authentic *backgrounds* and events.

HMSO: see *Her Majesty's Stationery Office*.

holding fee: *n* a fee charged by a supplier, *eg* a *picture agency*, for material held beyond the agreed borrowing time.

holograph: *n* a *manuscript* or *typescript* which includes corrections, alterations and additions. (Greek: 'whole writing'.)

home page: *n* the first *page* you come to when you log on to a *website*.

homonym: *n* a word with the same sound and possibly the same spelling as another word but with a different meaning and origin; *eg* the bark of a dog and the bark of a tree. (Greek: 'same name'.)

homophone: *n* a word which is pronounced the same as another but has a different spelling and meaning; *eg* bow/bough, peer/pier. (Greek: 'same sound'.)

honorarium: *n* a small token payment in money or in the form of a *credit* and/or copies of a *publication(2)* in which the writer's work appears.

hook: *n* a strong beginning, a catchy early sentence or *paragraph* designed to grip the *reader(1)'s* attention and tempt him to read on. (Stephen King calls it 'the gotcha'.)

horizontal format: *n* American for *landscape format*.

horror: *n* a *category* of literature emphasising fear, death, reincarnation, the occult, necromancy, vampirism and the macabre.

host: *n* the main computer on a system, allowing access to *websites* and *databases*.

hotspot: *n* a special area on an image or display which becomes active when the *cursor* is placed on it.

house: see *publishing house*.

house copy: *n* a copy of a *magazine* or book kept for use in the *publisher's* offices.

house corrections (*abbr* HCs): *n* corrections and alterations made by the *publisher* or printer, as distinct from those made by the *author*.

house editor: see under *editor*.

house magazine: *n* a *magazine* produced by a company for its employees, carrying company and staff news; *eg* 'Ariel', the *BBC* magazine. Also called *house organ*.

house organ: n same as *house magazine*.

house reader: *n* a *proofreader* employed *in-house* by a printing or publishing *house*.

house style: *n* the *style* of *punctuation*, spelling, *layout etc* which is specified by a *publishing house* to ensure *consistency* throughout its range of products.

how-dun-it?: *n* a mystery or crime story in which 'who-dun-it' is revealed early so that the interest lies in discovering how the crime was committed.

how-to: *n* a book or *article* giving detailed advice and practical working methods on a specific subject.

HTML: see *Hypertext Markup Language*.

http: see *hypertext transfer protocol*.

human interest material: *n* material about people, their achievements, problems, ambitions, social and economic circumstances *etc.*

humour: *n* writing designed to entertain by arousing amusement.

hype: *n slang abbr* of *hyperbole*.

hyped book: *n* a book which is 'talked up' to high sales by extravagant *promotion* and by hyperbolic *puffs* and *reviews* which exaggerate its worth.

hyperbole (*slang abbr* hype): *n* obvious and extravagant exaggeration. (Greek: 'throwing too far'.)

HyperText Markup Language (*abbr* HTML): the language in which *web* pages are written.

hypertext transfer protocol (*abbr* http): a series of commands used by a *browser* to ask an *Internet web server* for information about a *web page*.

hypotactic style: *n* the use of words like 'however' and 'because', and phrases like 'on the other hand', to show the connections between ideas; the opposite of *paratactic style*.

I

iamb: *n* a metrical *foot* consisting of an unstressed *syllable* followed by a stressed one.

ibidem (*abbr* ib or ibid): *adv* a Latin term used in *footnotes* and *bibliographies*, meaning 'to be found in the same place'.

icon: *n* 1. a *symbol(1)*, picture or representation. 2. a small image on a computer screen which activates a function when clicked. (Greek: 'image'.)

id: see *idem*.

idem (*abbr* id): Latin term meaning 'the same'.

id est (*abbr* ie): Latin term meaning 'that is'.

idiom: *n* a distinctive expression peculiar to a particular language or *dialect*. (Greek: 'peculiar phraseology'.)

idyll: *n* a *poem* with a rural and tranquil setting. (Greek: 'little picture'.)

ie: see *id est*.

illustration: *n* a drawing, painting, diagram or photograph reproduced to reinforce or decorate a description or argument.

illustrator: *n* an artist who originates *illustrations* to complement a *text(1)*.

image: *n* a picture or reflection.

imagery: *n* the use of language to evoke pictures in the imagination, and to clarify sensory experience, actions, ideas *etc.* (Latin: 'likeness'.) See *figures of speech*.

imperfect rhyme: *n* inexact *rhyme* between two words, *eg* roving/loving; also called *half-rhyme*.

imposition: *n* the arrangement of *pages* for printing, so that after folding they will read in sequence.

impression: *n* the number of copies of a book printed in a single *print run(1)*. A second and subsequent impression, where no changes have been made, is a *reprint*.

impressionistic writing: *n* writing which aims to convey meaning and emotion through phrases and fragments of *dialogue* or description, without the use of whole sentences. The writer relies on the *reader(1)'s* imagination to make the connections.

imprint: *n* 1. the printer's name, with the place and date of printing, required by law in many countries, including the UK, to be shown on published material. 2. the *publisher's* name with the place and date of *publication(2)*.

incantation: *n* words chanted or spoken to create a magical effect.

inciting incident: *n* the first major occurrence and *plot* point in a *story*.

incunabula: *pl n* books printed from movable *type* before 1501. (Latin: 'cradle'.)

indemnity: see *warranty*.

indent: *v* to *set* a line or lines to a shorter measure than the full *text(1)* width.

in-depth interview: *n* an *interview* which allows the interviewer to probe for detailed and authenticated information.

index: *n* an alphabetical list of subjects dealt with in a book, giving the number of every *page* where a reference to each subject appears.

indexer: *n* a person who compiles indexes.

indirect quote: *n* information quoted in its meaning but not *verbatim*; *eg* 'John said he would sue', as distinct from 'John said "I'll sue"', (direct quote).

indirect speech: *n* speech that doesn't appear in *quotation* *marks,* as spoken, but which is incorporated into the *narrative, eg* 'He said he wanted to go home', as distinct from 'He said "I want to go home"' (direct speech).

informative article: *n* an *article* which gives solid information, as distinct from *opinion* or conjecture.

infringement of copyright: *n* the unauthorised use of *copyright* material.

in-house: *adj* describes a service or process carried out by a company's own personnel, and not bought in from outside or contracted out.

initiating editor: see under *editor.*

in medias res: *n* a technique in which a *narrator* begins in the middle of a *story* rather than at the beginning; *eg* Emily Brontë's 'Wuthering Heights' (1848). (Latin: 'into the middle of things'.)

innovative fiction: *n fiction* which experiments with *form, structure* and language, trying new ways to express and convey meaning.

innuendo: *n* indirect reference or insinuation.

in print: *adj* 1. books and other *publications(2)* currently available. 2. the total number of copies printed since a book's first *publication(1).*

input: *n* information put into a computer memory.

insert: *n* additional *copy* to be included in work already written or *typeset.*

inset: *n* a *page* or pages included in a book or *magazine* but not an integral part of it, nor included in the *pagination.*

inspection copy: *n* a book sent free by *publishers* to teachers and academics with a view to securing *adoptions.*

inspirational writing: *n* writing that emphasises religious and moral values, written to inspire faith in such values; also called *brighteners.*

instalment: *n* a section of a book or *magazine* published at regular intervals.

instant publishing: *n* the publishing of books immediately after an event.

instructional article: *n* an *article* giving practical and detailed instruction about how to do or make something.

integrated services digital network (*abbr* ISDN): *n* a service that provides telecommunications, *eg* video conferencing.

intellectual property: *n* ideas, original writing, art, music, inventions *etc* which belong to their creator and are protected by *copyright* or patent.

interface: *n* the point at which two systems come in contact with each other.

interior monologue: *n* the expression of a *character's(1)* thoughts without the use of *dialogue* (unless it is 'remembered' dialogue).

Inter-Library Loan Service: *n* a service through which books can be borrowed from libraries outside a local area.

internal rhyme: *n* two or more words rhyming within a line of *poetry*.

International Reply Coupon (*abbr* IRC): a postal coupon exchangeable in most countries for stamps to the value of international surface-mail postage.

International Standard Book Number (*abbr* ISBN): a unique reference number given to every book published, to identify its area of origin and its *publisher*. Each new *edition* of a book is given a new ISBN.

International Standard Series Number (*abbr* ISSN): a reference number for *periodical publications(2)* in a system similar to the *ISBN*.

Internet: *n* a global collection of computer networks with a common addressing scheme.

Internet Explorer: *n* the most widely used *web browser*.

Internet service provider (*abbr* ISP): *n* an intermediary providing access to the *Internet*.

interview: *n* an *article* in the form of a conversation; might be told as a sequence of questions and answers, or *paraphrased* into an account of the conversation.

intranet: *n* a *website* designed to operate and be accessible only over a *network*.

intrigue: *n* secret dealings, deceit, and underhand plans in a *story*.

introduction (*abbr* intro): *n* 1. the opening section of a work, written by the *author* or by another person commenting on the work and/or the author. 2. the opening *paragraph* of a *feature* or *article*, possibly printed in bigger and/or bolder *type* than the body of the piece.

inverted pyramid: *n* a way of arranging material so that an *article* begins with the broadest and most important aspect. The rest of the material is added in descending order of importance so that the *reader(1)* gets the gist of the *piece* even if he doesn't read it all, and so that, if necessary, the article can be cut from the bottom up without losing important *facts.*

invoice: *n* a *document* listing goods or services provided and stating the amount of money owed for these.

IRC: see *International Reply Coupon.*

irony: *n* the conveyance of meaning by the use of words whose literal meaning is something quite different; usually satirical.

ISBN: see *International Standard Book Number.*

ISDN: see *Integrated Services Digital Network.*

isp: see *Internet Service Provider.*

ISSN: see *International Standard Series Number.*

issue: *n* all the copies of a *periodical* produced on one particular day.

issue life: *n* the time during which a *periodical* remains *topical.*

Italian sonnet: *n* another name for *Petrarchan sonnet.*

italic: *n* a *type* design with sloping letters, indicated in *typescript* by single underlining.

J

jacket: *n* a paper cover on a book.

jacket copy: *n* *matter* printed on a book *jacket,* such as the *blurb, puffs,* information about the *author etc.*

jargon: *n* words, phrases and *acronyms* common to a particular subject or occupation. (French: 'birdsong'.)

jeu d'esprit: *n* a short witty light-hearted *piece,* written for fun. (French: 'game of the mind'.)

jingle: *n* a simple light *rhyme,* like those used in television or radio *advertisements.*

joint authorship: see *collaboration.*

Joint Photographic Experts Group: see *JPEG.*

journal: *n* 1. a *periodical* usually covering a single subject or a group of related subjects. 2. a contemporary record of ideas, thoughts, impressions *etc.* (Old French: 'daily'.)

journalese: *n* a derogatory term applied to *cliché*-ridden writing.

journalism: *n* 1. the profession of writing for *journals(1), newspapers, magazines* and other *periodicals.* 2. material produced by such writing.

journalist: *n* a person who writes for *journals(1)*, *newspapers*, *magazines* and other *periodicals*.

journalistic eye: *n* the ability to recognise potential in a short news item that might be developed into a *feature*.

JPEG: *n* a *web* graphics *format* developed by the Joint Photographic Experts Group.

jump: *n* part of a *story* carried over to continue on a later but not the following *page*.

jumping viewpoint: *n* changes of *viewpoint* from one *character(1)* to another or several others in the same sequence of a *story*.

justification: see *justified setting*.

justified setting/justification: *n* the spacing out of words and *characters(2)* so that each line of *text(1)* is the same length, flush at left and right.

juvenile: *adj* a term commonly used to describe children's books.

juvenile biography: *n* a *biography* written for young readers, using simple, clear language with more action and *dialogue* than description and *exposition*.

juvenilia: *pl n* work written during an *author's* childhood. (Latin: 'youth-works'.)

K

kabuki: *n* a popular form of Japanese *drama*, often based on *myths* and *legends(1)*.

Kb: see *kilobyte*.

kern: *v* to make two *characters(2)* overlap.

key character: *n* the principal *character(1)*, the main *protagonist*, whose *motivations*, actions and reactions decide the course of a *story*.

key in: *v* to indicate the position of *illustrations* by marking their approximate location in the *margin* of a *typescript* or *proof*.

key letter: see *key number*.

key number/key letter: *n* a code in an advertiser's address identifying the *publication(2)* and *issue* which attracts the biggest response; *eg* 'J. Smith (ST2)' = 'J. Smith (Sunday Times 2nd insert)'. Sometimes disguised as a department, *eg* 'J. Smith (Dept ST2)'.

keystroke: *n* a single operation of a key on a computer keyboard.

keyword: *n* a word used by a *search engine* to find a particular *website*.

keyword and context (*abbr* KWAC): *n* a library indexing system which uses words from the *title(1)* and *text(1)* as the *index* entries.

keyword in context (*abbr* KWIC): *n* a library indexing system which uses the *title(1)* or *text(1)* to show the meaning of the *index* entry.

keyword out of context (*abbr* KWOC): *n* a library indexing system which uses any relevant *keywords*, not necessarily words from the *text(1)*.

keyword out of title (*abbr* KWOT): *n* a library indexing system which uses words not in the *title(1)*.

kill: *v* to scrap material that is no longer wanted, *eg* a *feature* that has become out of date or an *illustration* for which no space can be found.

kill fee: *n* a fee paid to a writer when, through no fault of theirs, a *commissioned piece* has been rejected ('killed') after it has been completed. Might also be applied to work accepted though not originally commissioned.

kilobyte (*abbr* Kb): *n* a unit of measurement for data storage, equals 1.024 *bytes*.

kitchen sink drama: *n* a term applied to plays and films of the 1950s and 1960s which focused on the problems of everyday domestic life, *eg* the works of John Osborne and Arnold Wesker.

knocking copy: *n advertising* material that contains criticism of competing products.

künstlerroman: *n* a *novel* about the development of an artist or writer, *eg* James Joyce's 'A Portrait of the Artist as a Young Man' (1916). (German: 'artist-novel'.)

KWAC: see *keyword and context*.

KWIC: see *keyword in context*.

KWOC: see *keyword out of context*.

KWOT: see *keyword out of title*.

kyrielle: *n* a French form of *poetry* dating from the Middle Ages, often used in hymns. Written in *couplet* or *quatrain stanzas*, it has a *refrain* in the last line of each stanza, the refrain being part- or whole-line; couplet *rhyme scheme*, aabBccbB, four-line rhyme scheme, abaBcbcB. *Eg* in couplet form

Dim shadows, moving through the past
jolt me, and memories flooding fast
swamp all my thoughts. I fix my eye
beyond the clouds to dark, full sky.

No man shall ever touch my dreams;
my veins bleed dust of arid streams.
No man shall ever hear my cry
beyond the clouds to dark, full sky . . .
(© Alison Chisholm)

L

lad's mag: *n* a *magazine* aimed at young men, focusing on cars, bands, sport, gadgets and girls.

lament: *n* a *poem* expressing deep sorrow.

lampoon: *n* a vicious *satire*. (French: 'let us swig'.)

landscape: *n* horizontal *format*, a *page* or *illustration* wider than it is deep; also called *oblong*.

layout: *n* 1. an *outline* sketching the appearance of a finished *page*, showing the planned relationship of *text(1)*, *display matter* and *illustrations*. 2. the over-all appearance of a book or *magazine's* text and illustrations.

lc: see *lower case*.

lead: *n* in *journalism*, refers to the opening of a news *story* or *magazine article*.

lead character: *n* same as *key character*.

lead time: *n* the time between the *copy date* and the date of *publication(1)*.

lead title: *n* the book a *publisher* selects to be the most heavily promoted in a season, and on which the biggest slice of the *advertising* budget will be spent.

leader: *n* 1. an *editorial(1)*. 2. a principal *piece*, a main *story* or *article* in a *newspaper* or *magazine*. 3. a group of dots (usually three) leading into a piece of material, or placed to lead the eye across the *page*.

leading: *n* the white space between lines of *type*; from the days of hot lead type.

leaf: *n* a single sheet of paper comprising two *pages* back to back.

learned journal: *n* a specialist academic *magazine*.

legal deposit: *n* a legal requirement in the UK; *publishers* must send six copies of every *title(2)* they produce that has an *ISBN* or *ISSN* number to the British National Book Collection for distribution to the British Library Archives, Cambridge University Library, the Bodleian Library at Oxford, and the National Libraries of Scotland, Wales and Ireland.

legend: *n* 1. a traditional *story*, not historically verified and probably untrue. 2. a term for a *caption*. (Latin: 'that which is read'.)

legibility: *n* the clarity of material, the ease with which it can be read.

letter narration: *n* a *story* told in the form of a letter or series of letters; also called *epistolary narration*.

letter of enquiry: *n* a preliminary letter to an *editor*, *publisher* or agent asking if they would be interested in seeing a particular *piece* of work.

letter space: *n* the space between two *typeset* letters.

letterpress: *n* printing from raised inked *characters(2)*, the oldest method of printing.

lexicography: *n* the compiling and writing of a dictionary.

lexicon: *n* a dictionary, especially of Latin or Greek words. (Greek: 'concerning words'.)

libel: *n* a statement written, printed or broadcast in any medium, defaming an identifiable living person by holding them up to hatred, ridicule or contempt.

library binding: *n* reinforced binding strong enough to withstand much handling.

library material: *n illustrations* or *text(1)* kept on file for future use.

library picture/library shot: *n* a photograph or other *illustration* from an existing source, as distinct from one that is *commissioned*.

library shot: see *library picture*.

library supplier: *n* a company which sources books and sells them to libraries.

libretto: *n* the *text(1)* of a work involving words and music. (Italian: 'little book'.)

licence period: *n* the period of time, usually clearly defined in a *contract*, for which an *author* grants a *publisher* agreed *rights*.

light verse: *n verse* not intended to be taken seriously.

limerick: *n* a five-line *poem*, often light-hearted or comic, *rhyme scheme* aabba; *eg*

There was a young lady of Clyde
'Twas of eating green apples she died
The apples fermented
Inside the lamented
And made cider inside her inside.
(Edward Lear, 1812–88).

limited edition: *n* an *edition* of a book where a fixed number of copies is produced and numbered, with a guarantee that no more copies of that edition will be made.

limited narrator: *n* a *narrator* whose view of events is limited to their own personal knowledge and which therefore must be incomplete.

limp binding: *n* any binding without *boards*, especially a *paperback* binding.

linage/lineage: *n* 1. the number of lines in a piece of printed matter. 2. measurement or payment by the line.

line art: *n* line drawings, *cartoons* and the like, as distinct from photographs.

line editor: see under *editor*.

line measure: *n* the length of a line of *typeset characters(2)*.

line space: *n* a line of blank space between lines of *type*, equivalent to one line of *typesetting*. Usually indicates a break in the *text(1)*.

linguistics: *n* the scientific study of language.

link: *n* 1. a phrase that links a *paragraph* to the preceding one, giving a smooth flow of reading, *eg* 'On the other hand . . .', 'As a result of that . . .'. 2. with reference to *web pages*, a word or phrase that, when selected, sends the user to a different page or *website*.

list: *n* 1. a *publisher's catalogue*. 2. *titles(2)* which a *publisher* offers for sale, both *back list* and new titles. 3. titles which a *publisher* produces in a season, *eg* his 'Spring List'.

list article: *n* an *article* consisting of a list of information or advice, *eg* 'Ten Tips to Trim Your Budget'.

list price/cover price: *n* the price at which a book or other *publication(2)* is offered for sale to the public and against which *trade discounts* are made.

literal (US typo): *n* a *typesetter's* error. The equivalent of a typing error, usually involving only one or two *characters(2)*.

literary agent: *n* a person who acts on behalf of *authors*, offering their work to *publishers* and negotiating *contracts*. Normally works on commission only, usually 10%–15% of the author's earnings on work the agent places.

literary fiction: *n fiction* which is generally considered to be of higher quality than *genre fiction*.

literary magazine: *n* a *magazine* publishing 'fine writing': *essays*, literary *criticism*, literary and *experimental fiction*, *reviews etc*, as distinct from 'popular' reading.

literary mash-up: *n* a sub-*genre* in which an out-of-*copyright literary novel* is mixed with another genre, *eg* the 2009 novel 'Pride & Prejudice and Zombies' by Jane Austen and Seth Grahame-Smith.

literary novel: *n* usually accepted to mean a high quality *novel* that can't be categorised in any *genre*.

literary scout: *n* a person, who might be a *freelance* or who might be employed by an *agent* or *publisher*, who looks out for writers that agents might want to represent and for books with the potential to make profits and/or to set trends.

literary work: *n* work entirely conveyed by written means.

literature of the absurd: *n* writing focused on the essential absurdity of the human condition *eg* Franz Kafka's 'Metamorphosis' (1916).

litotes: *n* a *figure of speech* in which something positive is expressed in a negative way, *eg* 'John is no mean artist'. (Greek: 'meagre'.)

little magazine: *n* a *literary magazine* run by enthusiasts (often one person), sometimes serving special interest or experimental writing; almost invariably struggling for financial survival.

local colour: *n* characteristics and peculiarities of a particular region or locality, used as *background* for a story – its geography, *dialect*, customs, attitudes, modes of dress *etc*.

local interest title: *n* a book which is of interest to people living in or visiting a particular area.

local newspaper: *n* a *newspaper* almost exclusively concerned with news and *features* about its local community.

location: *n* the place in which the action of a *story* is set.

logo: *n abbr* of 'logotype', a trade mark or design. See also *colophon*.

long complete story: *n* a *story* longer than the *short stories* a *magazine* usually publishes but complete in itself and not part of a *serial* story.

loose leaf: *n* a binding which allows *pages* to be inserted or removed.

lullaby: *n* a song sung to a child to send it to sleep. (Latin: 'to sing'.)

lower case (*abbr* lc): *n* small letters as distinct from *capitals*. So-called because in the days when *type* was *set* by hand, the small letters were kept in a case below the *upper case*, the case that held the capital letters.

lyric poetry: *n* relatively short *poetry* usually expressing personal feelings.

lyrics: *n* the words of songs.

M

macaronic verse: *n* *verse* made up of languages muddled together for comic effect; often used in *nonsense verse*. (From the Italian food 'maccheroni'.)

machine binding: *n* binding by an automatic binding machine.

madrigal: *n* a *lyric poem* about love or the pastoral life, intended to be sung.

magazine: *n* a *periodical publication(2),* usually weekly or monthly. (Arabic: 'storehouse'.)

magazine supplement: *n* a *magazine* sold with a *newspaper* and included in the price.

magnum opus: *n* a writer's greatest work. (Latin: 'great work'.)

mail merge: *n* a word processing *program* which lets you send a standard letter to different names and addresses.

mail shot: *n* information sent by mail to possible customers.

mailing list: *n* a list of names and addresses kept by an organisation or an individual.

mainstream: *n* literature that is traditional or current, as distinct from *category* or *genre* work.

majuscule: *n* a *capital* or *upper case* letter.

make even: *n* to arrange *type* so that it runs the full width of the line.

make up: *v* to make up *typeset* material into *pages*, including *text(1), running heads, footnotes, illustrations etc.*

malware: *n* *software, eg* viruses, intended to damage computer systems.

manga: *n* a Japanese style of comic-book drawing.

manilla: *n* strong thick brown paper used in the manufacture of tear-resistant envelopes.

mannerism: *n* a recurring feature in a writer's work.

manual: *n* an instructional *handbook* or *document*.

manual of style: see *Chicago Manual of Style*.

manuscript (*abbr* ms, *pl* mss): *n* hand-written, typewritten or word-processed *text(1)*. (Latin: 'written by hand'.)

marbling: *n* coloured patterns used to decorate *endpapers*.

margin: *n* the space above, below and on either side of the *text(1)*.

margin guide: *n* in *desktop publishing programs*, a non-printing line or box that shows the position of the margins on-screen.

marginalia: *pl n* material printed or written in the *margin*, usually commenting on the *text(1)*.

mark up: *v* to mark the *manuscript* with instructions (design, *typography etc*) for the *typesetter* or printer.

marked proof: *n* 1. a *proof* supplied to the *author* for correction; ideally, this should be marked already with corrections and queries made by the *typesetter's proofreader*. 2. a *proof* on which all corrections (typesetter's, editor's and author's) are marked; sometimes called the *master proof*.

market: 1. *n* the publishing businesses that constitute an *author's* possible points of sale. 2. *v* to offer or to sell work to a *publisher*.

market analysis: see *market research, market study*.

market research: *n* study of the *market(1)* to identify the most likely point(s) of sale for a particular work.

market study: *n* detailed analysis of the *market(1)* to assess content, *style* and *readership*.

marketable: *adj* easy to sell.

masculine rhyme: *n* a monosyllabic *rhyme* on the last stressed *syllables* in two lines of *verse, eg*

Humpty Dumpty sat on a wall
Humpty Dumpty had a great fall.

mash-up: *n* a combination of two different *genres*. See *literary mash-up*.

mass market paperback: *n* a *paperback* cheaply produced, usually with a substantial *print run*.

master: *n* an original *document* from which copies are made.

master file: *n* the main copy of a computer *file*, kept for security purposes.

master proof: see *marked proof(2)*.

masthead: *n* 1. the *title(1)* of a *publication(2)* prominently printed on the cover of each *issue*. 2. a block of information about a *publication(2)'s* contents. 3. a list of people who work on a *publication*(2), with their work titles.

matter: *n* a term applied to a *manuscript* or other *copy* to be *typeset*, or *type* that is *set* for printing.

maxim: *n* a short pithy statement about how life should be lived. (Latin: 'proposition'.)

mb: see *megabit*.

MB: see *megabyte*.

mbps: see *megabits per second*.

MBS: see *mind, body and spirit*.

Mbyte: see *megabyte*.

measure: *n* 1. the width of a line of *type*. 2. another word for *metre*.

media: *n* information sources like *newspapers*, *magazines*, radio, television, *Internet* news services *etc*; plural of medium, *ie* 'medium of communication'. (Latin: 'means'.)

media guide: *n* a *guide* to companies and *publications(2)* in the *media*; *eg* 'Willing's Press Guide'.

media pack: *n* a package of information about a *publication(2)* giving details of its *circulation* and *readership*, and possibly its forthcoming content, to attract *advertising*.

megabit (*abbr* mb): *n* one million bits.

megabits per second (*abbr* mbps): *n* a measure of the speed of data transfer.

megabyte (*abbr* MB, Mbyte): *n* a computer storage unit roughly equivalent to one million printed *characters(2)*.

melodrama: *n* a work (usually a play) that relies on improbable events, sensational incidents and exaggerated reactions. (Greek: 'song-play'.)

memento mori: *n* an emblem of death, *eg* a skull, to remind us of the precariousness of life. (Latin: 'Remember you must die'.)

memo: *n* a short message from one person to another in the same organisation; *abbr* of 'memorandum'.

memoir: *n* an account of people and events a person has known in life; less personal and detailed than an *autobiography*. (French: 'memory'.)

men's fiction: *n fiction* (usually *short stories*) in which *erotica*, *adventure* and *suspense* are predominant.

menu: *n* a list of options displayed on a computer screen.

merchandising: see *character merchandising*.

metadata: *pl n* essential information contained in a *web page* or *document*, such as its *author, title(1), publication date, keywords* and summary, enabling it to be found by *search engines*.

metafiction: *n fiction* whose subject is fiction itself, and which keeps reminding us that we are reading fiction, thus never allowing *suspension of disbelief*; see *eg* John Fowles's *novel* 'The French Lieutenant's Woman' (1969).

metaphor: *n* a *figure of speech* in which something is represented as being something else, *eg* 'Life is just a bowl of cherries'. (Greek: 'a carrying over'.) See also *mixed metaphor*.

metonymy: *n* a *figure of speech* in which a word or phrase is substituted for something it represents, *eg* 'Downing Street' for the Prime Minister, 'the turf' for horse racing. (Greek: 'change of name'.)

metre: *n* structured *rhythm* in the arrangement of *syllables*. Usually applied to *poetry* but can also be used effectively in *prose*. (Greek: 'measure'.)

mf: *abbr* of 'more follows', a term used in *manuscript* and *copy preparation* to indicate that there is more matter to come on the following *page(s)*; usually typed at the bottom of every manuscript page except the last, where 'ends' should appear below the last line.

microfiche: *n* a small sheet of photographic film on which information is stored in tiny print.

microfiche reader: *n* a machine that magnifies the information on *microfiche* film, enabling it to be read on a monitor.

microfilter: *n* a device attached to your telephone socket enabling voice and data calls to be made at the same time via *ADSL*.

Microsoft Internet Explorer: *n* a *web browser program* supplied by Microsoft.

Microsoft Network (*abbr* MSN): *n* a vast online service providing information, database *links* to the *Internet* and *electronic mail* services for Windows users.

Microsoft Outlook Express: *n* an *e-mail* handling *program* supplied by Microsoft.

midlist: *adj* describes books that sell reasonably well but don't make the *bestseller* lists; also applied to *authors* of such books.

Mind, body and spirit (*abbr* **MBS**): *n* a category of books dealing with topics like natural medicine, holistic healing, new faiths, Oriental mysticism *etc.*

mini-article: *n* a very short *article*, about 300-800 words.

Minimum Terms Agreement (MTA): *n* an *agreement* designed to clarify (and possibly eventually to standardise) the terms of *contract* between *authors* and *publishers*. Drafted and negotiated by *The Society of Authors* and the *Writers' Guild of Great Britain*, the MTA's standards are now accepted by a growing number of publishers, including some of the major *houses.*

mint: *adj* unused and in perfect condition.

mint stock: *n* stock which is new and in perfect condition.

minuscule: *n* a small or *lower case* letter.

miscellany: *n* a collection of writings about different subjects by different *authors*; might be a variety of pieces with some connection such as having been published in the same *magazine* series.

misery memoir: *n* a personal story dwelling on its *author's* unhappy life experiences.

misprint: *n* a mistake in printing.

mission statement: *n* a statement of aims and objectives.

mixed metaphor: *n* a *metaphor* that combines two or more metaphoric ideas, giving an effect, usually unintended, of absurd incongruity; *eg* 'Putting his shoulder to the wheel, he jumped in at the deep end.'

mix: *v* to use different *fonts* and *typefaces* in the same line.

MO: see *modus operandi.*

mock-heroic: *adj* describes any work which treats a trivial subject with seriousness.

mock-up: *n* a roughly made *dummy.*

model release: *n* a form to be signed by the subject of a photograph giving *permission* for that photograph to be used for commercial purposes.

modem: *n* a device that connects a computer to the *Internet* via a telephone line.

modus operandi (*abbr* **MO**): *n* a Latin term meaning 'method of working'; often used in *crime fiction*, especially *police procedural novels*, describing criminal activities.

monitor: *n* a visual display unit for showing material generated by a computer.

monodrama: *n* a dramatic work for one actor playing one *character(1)*. (Greek: 'alone-play'.)

monogram: *n* a device made up of several initials linked together.

monograph: *n* a *publication(2)* usually short, dealing with a single subject.

monologue: *n* a composition intended to be spoken aloud by one person. (Greek: 'speaking alone'.)

montage: *n* a combination of drawings, photographs, or parts of pictures used for display or *advertising*.

monthly: *n* a *magazine* published every month.

mood: see *atmosphere*.

Moral Rights: *n* introduced in the Copyright, Designs and Patents Act of 1988, Moral Rights complement but do not supersede *copyright*. It gives the writer the right to be identified as the *author* of their own work and prevents anyone else from distorting or mutilating that work. However, unlike the rest of Europe, where Moral Rights is undisputed and automatic, in the UK it must be asserted in writing, otherwise it is deemed not to exist.

'more follows': see *mf*.

morgue: *n* a *newspaper* reference library.

morocco: *n* a fine leather goatskin used in binding.

motif: *n* a recurring element, moral or principle that gives depth and cohesion to a *story*.

motion picture rights: *n* same as *film rights*.

motivation: *n* the physical, emotional or psychological needs that drive a *character(1)*.

motive: *n* the reason or incentive for an action.

mouse: *n* a small hand device for controlling the *cursor* on a computer screen.

mouse potato: *n* the computer equivalent of a couch potato.

Moving Picture Experts Group (*abbr* MPEG): *n* a data file for moving pictures on the *Internet*.

Moving Picture Experts Group, Audio Layer 3 (*abbr* MP3): *n* a computer *file* standard for downloading compressed music from the *Internet*.

MP3: see *Moving Picture Experts Group, Audio Layer 3*.

.mp3: *n* an extension for an MP3 file.

MPEG: *see Moving Picture Experts Group.*

.mpeg: a *file* extension for an MPEG file.

ms: see *manuscript.*

MSN: *see* Microsoft Network.

MTA: see *Minimum Terms Agreement.*

multicolumn layout: *n* a *page layout* with several *columns(1)*, as used in *magazines* and *newspapers.*

multi-disk reader: *n* a device that reads data from different sizes and *formats* of *disk.*

multimedia: *pl n programs*, *software* and *hardware* that can use a variety of *media* like music, film and video as well as *text(1)* and numbers.

multiple submission: *n* more than one *submission* sent to the same *market(1)* at the same time. See *simultaneous submission.*

multiple viewpoint: *n* the use of the *viewpoints* of more than one *narrator* to tell a *story.*

multitask: *v* to run several different *programs* at the same time.

muse: *n* inspiration derived from the nine daughters of Zeus and Mnemosyne, each of whom presides over a separate activity:

Calliope	epic poetry
Erato	love poetry
Melpomene	tragedy
Thalia	comedy
Clio	history
Euterpe	lyric poetry
Terpsichore	dancing
Urania	astronomy
Polyhymnia	songs of praise to the gods

Mystery: *n* a *story* in which one or more elements remain unexplained till the end.

Mystery plays: *n* plays of the Middle Ages that recreated an incident or action from the Bible.

myth: *n* 1. an ancient traditional *story* involving gods, heroes and/or supernatural beings, often explaining a *fact* or phenomenon. 2. *n* a common belief that has no true foundation. (Greek: 'something uttered by word of mouth'.)

mythology: *n* the study of *myths.*

N

narration: *n* the telling of a *story*; an account of a series of events. (Latin: 'telling'.)

narrative: *n* a *story*.

narrative poem: *n* a *story* told in the form of a long *poem*, *eg* John Milton's 'Paradise Lost' (1667).

narrative verse: *n* same as *narrative poem*.

narrator: *n* a person who tells a *story*, or from whose *viewpoint* a story is told. See also *viewpoint character*.

narrow measure: *n type* that is *set* in narrow widths, usually in *columns(1)*.

National Book League: see *Book Trust*.

national media: *pl n* nationally distributed broadcast and print products.

national newspaper: *n* a *newspaper* whose circulation covers the whole country and which carries national and international *news*.

national press: *n national newspapers*.

National Union of Journalists (*abbr* NUJ): *n* a British trade union whose members work in *newspaper* and book publishing, and in radio and television.

navigate: *v* to move around the different areas of a *website* using the links provided.

NBA: see *Net Book Agreement*.

nd: *abbr* of 'no date', used in *bibliographies* with reference to books that show no *publication date*.

ne: see *new edition*.

neckline: *n* a blank line under a *headline*.

nemesis: *n* the deserved punishment that inevitably comes to the tragic *hero*. (Greek: 'retribution'.)

neologism: *n* an innovation in language; an invented word. (Greek: 'new word'.)

.net: *n Internet domain name* indicating an organisation that is connected to the operation of the *Internet*.

net: *adj* with no discount allowed.

net book: *n* a book whose retail price is fixed.

Net Book Agreement (*abbr* NBA): an agreement in the publishing and bookselling trades that books will be sold to the public at the retail price stipulated by their *publisher*; no longer in effect in the UK.

netiquette: *n* unwritten rules governing what is and what is not acceptable activity on the *Internet*.

netlag: *n* a temporary loss of connection between a user and an *Internet server*.

net receipts: *n* the amount received by a *publisher* after the deduction of discounts and commissions.

net royalty: *n* a *royalty* based on the actual amount of money a *publisher* receives after deductions for discounts and *returns*.

network: *n* a large number of people, organisations or machines that work together as a system.

new edition (*abbr* ne): *n* a book that has been reprinted with changes and updating.

New Hart's Rules: The Handbook of Style for Writers and Editors (the University Press, Oxford): *n* a *manual* of guidance on spelling, *punctuation* and hyphenation widely used by *editors*, printers and *publishers* in the UK. The US equivalent is *The Chicago Manual of Style*.

new release: *n* a new book just launched on the retail market.

news: *n* information about things that have just happened.

news agency: *n* an organisation that collects news *stories* as they break and sells them on to *newspapers*, *periodicals*, radio and television companies.

news aggregator: *n* a service that gathers *headlines* from news-related sites and *blogs*.

newsgroup: *n* a discussion forum on the *Internet*.

newsletter: *n* a printed sheet or *pamphlet* circulating *news* in a company, a club, a group of people, a district and the like.

newspaper: *n* a regular *publication(2)*, usually daily or weekly, reporting and commenting on current *news*.

newsprint: *n* cheap paper for printing *newspapers*, *mass-market paperbacks etc.*

news release: *n* an information sheet about an event, sent to *newspapers* and to radio and television stations so that they can publicise it.

next to editorial: *n* an instruction from an advertiser to a *magazine* to place an *advertisement* next to *editorial* material and not among other adverts.

niche market: *n* a specialist *market(1)* usually offering limited sales potential.

noh: *n* Japanese *drama* of the fourteenth century, intended for an aristocratic audience, in contrast to the popular *kabuki*.

nom de plume: *n* French for 'pen name'. See *pseudonym*.

non-book: *n* a scornful term applied to a book designed to appeal to those who buy books as decorative objects rather than as reading matter.

nonce-word: *n* a word coined for a specific occasion and used only once. (Middle English: 'for-a-purpose word'.)

non-consumable textbook: *n* a *textbook* that students are required to keep clean and not to write in, so that it can be passed on for others to use.

non-fiction: *n* material dealing exclusively with reality – *facts*, views, opinions, true experiences and so on.

non-fiction novel: *n* a true *story* written in the form of a *novel*. Openly uses real names, events, *settings(2) etc*; *eg* Thomas Keneally's 'Schindler's Ark' (1982), filmed as 'Schindler's List'.

non-net book: *n* a book that may be sold at a price lower than that fixed by the *publisher*.

nonsense verse: *n verse* that is designed to amuse; *eg*

> Calico pie,
> The little birds fly
> Down to the calico tree,
> Their wings were blue,
> And they sang 'Tilly-loo! . . .
> (Edward Lear).

nostalgia: *n* writing which recalls the past fondly and wistfully, inviting the *reader(1)* to share the writer's memories of 'how things were'. (Greek: 'nostos' and 'algos', 'a return' and 'pain'.)

notice: *n* a written announcement displayed so that everyone can read it.

noun: *n* a word used as the name of a person, thing, animal, place, or quality.

novel: *n* a fictional *prose story*, not usually less than 50,000 words.

novelette: *n* a lightweight *novella*.

novella: *n* a short *novel*, of no fixed length, somewhere between a *long complete story* and a *novel*. (Italian: 'tale, news'.)

np: *abbr* of 'new paragraph', an instruction to the *typesetter*.

NUJ: see *National Union of Journalists*.

numbered edition: *n* a *limited edition* in which every copy has a number written in it.

numeral: a figure (1, 2, 3 *etc*) used to express a number.

nursery rhymes: *n verses* purported to be for children but which often have a more sinister source. *Eg*

> Ring-a-ring o' roses,
> A pocket full of posies,
> Achoo!, Achoo!
> We all fall down.

This first appeared in the 1881 book 'Mother Goose', but is actually an older chant from the 1660s about the Plague of London which killed 70,000 of the 460,000 residents. 'Ring-a-ring o' roses' refers to the rosy rash which is an early symptom of the plague. 'Pocket full of posies' refers to the herbs people carried to prevent the plague. 'Achoo! Achoo! We all fall down' refers to the last sneezes of those who died. See 'The Oxford Book of Nursery Rhymes' (1951) by Iona and Peter Opie.

'Nuts-and-bolts' article or book: *n* a practical basic *instructional* work.

O

obelisk: *n* the *symbol(1)* † used as a reference mark for a *footnote*. Also used after a person's name to indicate that he or she has died.

obituary (*abbr* obit): *n* an *article* in a *newspaper* about the life and work of a person who has recently died.

objective: *n* the *protagonist's* goal or desire in a *story*, the motivation for their actions.

objective viewpoint: *n* a *viewpoint* which presents the facts impartially, without emotion or opinion.

oblique: 1. *adj* indirect and hard to understand. 2. *n* the stroke /.

oblong: *n* another term for *landscape format*.

obscene: *adj* shocking or offensive.

obscenity: *n matter* considered likely to deprave and corrupt those who might read it. (It is an offence to publish such matter.)

obstacle: *n* a *plot* element that stands in the way of the *protagonist* achieving their goal.

occasional verse: *n verse* written to celebrate or commemo-rate a specific occasion, *eg* a royal birth.

octave: *n* 1. the first eight lines of a *sonnet*. 2. a *stanza* of eight lines.

octosyllabic couplet: *n* a rhymed *couplet* of eight-*syllable* lines, usually *iambic. Eg*

> Had we World enough, and Time,
> This coyness, Lady, were no crime. . . .
> ('To his Coy Mistress' (1681) by Andrew Marvell.)

odd pages: *n* the *pages* with odd numbers, *ie* the right-hand pages in a book.

ode: *n* a long lyrical *poem*, usually in praise of someone or something. (Greek: 'song'.)

off-centre: *n* not in the centre of a *page* or line.

offline: *n* not connected to a computer *network*.

offprint: *n* part of a *publication(2)*, *eg* an *article* or a *chapter* from a book, reprinted and produced as a separate item.

omission: *n* something that has been left out.

omnibus: *n* a book containing reprints of several works by the same *author* or on the same subject.

omniscient viewpoint: *n* the *narrator* as the all-seeing eye, showing the *reader(1)* more than any one *character(1)* can know; enables the *author* to manipulate the reader's knowledge of events, characters and other elements of the *story*.

on air/on the air: *n* being broadcast.

on-demand publishing: *n* a system enabling the printing of books in very small quantities as required.

on spec: see *on speculation*.

on speculation (*abbr* **on spec**): *n* a term applied to mate-rial submitted to an *editor* on a speculative basis, *ie* not invited or *commissioned*. Also applied to work sent at an editor's invitation but without any commitment on the editor's part. See also *unsolicited submission*.

one line break: *n* a *line space* between *paragraphs* in the same *chapter*, indicating a break in the sequence of events. Often used as a device to indicate a change of time or *location*.

one-off: *n* done once only.

one-shot rights: see *one-time rights*.

one time rights/one shot rights: *n* the *right* to publish a piece of work in one particular *issue* of a *publication(2)*; *permission* would be required for any further *publication(1)* of that work.

onion-skin: *n* very thin slippery paper, notoriously difficult to handle.

online: *n* connected to the *Internet*.

online storage: *n* data stored on the *Internet*.

Online Writing Lab: see *OWL*.

onomatopoeia: *n* the use of words whose sound echoes their meaning; *eg* 'buzzing bees', 'soft slushy snow'; sometimes called 'echoism'. (Greek: 'name-making'.)

op cit: see *opera citato*.

op-ed: *n abbr* of 'opinion-editorial', an *opinion piece* which appears on or near the *editorial(1) page* of a *newspaper* or *magazine*.

open-source: *n software* or information that is free to access, use, copy or distribute without licensing or *copyright* restriction.

opera citato (*abbr* op cit): *adv* a Latin phrase meaning 'in the work cited', used along with the *author's* name to refer to the same book as quoted in a previous reference.

operating system: *n* the *software* that manages your computer.

opinion piece: *n* an *article* in which the writer looks at a topic from a personal, possibly controversial, *point of view*.

option clause: *n* a clause in a *contract* giving a *publisher* first refusal of an *author's* next book or books.

oral tradition: *n* cultural material and stories transmitted by word of mouth from generation to generation.

oration: *n* a formal speech for a public occasion. (Latin: 'discourse'.)

.org: *n* an *Internet domain name* indicating a non-profit organisation.

original: *n artwork* or *copy* created (originated) for the purpose of being reproduced.

original paperback: *n* a book published in *paperback* without having been published in *hardback*.

originality: *n* the ability to create out of the ordinary.

origination: *n* all the processes in the preparation of *original* material for publishing, from *manuscript* and *artwork* to *typesetting*.

orphan: *n* the first line of a *paragraph* appearing at the foot of a *page*. See also *widow*.

ottava rima: *n* a *stanza* which comprises eight *iambic* lines, with the rhyming scheme ababbabcc. See *eg* 'Sailing to Byzantium' by William Butler Yeats (1865-1939). (Italian: 'eighth rhyme'.)

out of print: *n* no longer on the *publisher's list*, with all stock sold and no plans for reprinting.

outbox: *n* a location in an *e-mail program* designed to hold outgoing messages until they are sent out.

outline: *n* a complete sketched-out *structure* showing what an *article* or book will contain and in what order, but without detail.

outright payment: *n* a *one-off* payment where the *publisher* buys *all rights* from the *author*, with no *royalty* arrangement.

outsert: *n* an item, usually promotional, attached or banded to the outside of a *periodical*.

outside reader: *n* a *reader(2)* who is not an employee but who might be either an expert in their field or someone experienced in publishing who is engaged by a *publisher* to evaluate and comment on *manuscripts*.

outsource: *v* to send work outside a company to be done by another company or by *freelancers*.

outwork: *n* work such as editing or design commissioned by a *publisher* but undertaken off the publisher's premises.

over the transom: *n* the American equivalent of the *slush pile;* slang for the arrival 'via the fanlight' of *unsolicited manuscripts*.

overlay: *n* a protective transparent sheet covering a photo or other *illustration*.

overprint: *v* to print over an area that has already been printed.

over-run: *n* 1. words run over from one line to the next, or for several successive lines, to accommodate an alteration that is longer than the material it replaces. 2. copies of a *publication(2)* printed in excess of the number specified.

overview: *n* the first part of a book *proposal*, describing the book and its potential *market(1)*.

OWL (Purdue University Online Writing Lab): *n* a comprehensive free-to-access resource for writers (http://owl.english.purdue.edu/).

own brand book: *n* a book specially packaged for a retailer, with the retailer's name printed on it.

oxymoron: *n* a contradiction in terms; *eg* Milton's description of hell: 'no light, but rather darkness visible' (Paradise Lost' (1667). (Greek: 'pointedly foolish'.)

P

PA: see *Publishers Association*.

pace: *n* the speed and *rhythm* of a *story*.

package deal: *n* an *agreement* covering several different items, *eg* '*paperback rights* plus *film and television rights*'.

packager: *n* a company that takes a book concept to a *publisher* and then oversees the funding and creation of the project; the resulting product is then released by the publisher. Payment is usually a *flat fee* for the idea and/or the writing, although further fees might be negotiated for reprints and/or foreign language *editions*.

pad out: *v* to add *text(1)* to make an *article* or a book longer.

padding: *n* material incorporated for the sole purpose of expanding a work; disliked by *editors* and difficult to disguise.

paean: *n* a song or *poem* of joy, triumph or exaltation; originally a hymn to Apollo. (Greek: 'striking'.)

page: *n* a single side of a sheet of paper.

page head: *n* a *running head*.

page make-up: *n* the assembly of all *text(1)*, *illustrations etc* into the final design and *layout* on the *page*.

page number: *n* the number shown on a *page* of a book or *magazine*.

page proofs: *n proofs* in which the *typeset* material has been divided into *pages* and the proofs of those pages (possibly without *illustrations*) collated in the order in which they will appear in the finished book.

page rate: *n* a method of payment at a fixed rate per printed *page*, regardless of *wordage*.

page reference: *n* a *cross-reference* to *text(1)* on a specific *page*.

pagination: *n page* numbering.

palaeography: *n* the study of ancient methods of writing, *manuscripts*, inscriptions. (Greek: 'ancient writing'.)

palette: *n* the range of colours available on a printer or computer display.

palimpsest: *n* a piece of parchment or other material which has been written on, rubbed out, and written on again many times, as in ancient days when materials were rare and expensive. (Greek: 'rubbed smooth again'.)

palindrome: *n* a word or phrase that reads the same forward and back; *eg* 'A man, a plan, a canal – Panama'. (Greek: 'running back again'.)

pamphlet: *n* a small-*format publication(2)* with only a few *pages*.

panegyric: *n* a speech or *essay* in praise of someone or something specific.

pantomime: *n* a U.K. theatrical entertainment, often based on a *nursery rhyme* or *fairy tale* and performed around Christmas-time. (Greek: 'all-imitator'.)

paper sizes (metric):

A0	841 mm x 1189 mm
A1	594 mm x 841 mm
A2	420 mm x 594 mm
A3	297 mm x 420 mm
A4	210 mm x 297 mm
A5	148 mm x 210 mm
A6	105 mm x 148 mm
A7	74 mm x 105 mm
A8	52 mm x 74 mm
A9	37 mm x 52 mm
A10	26 mm x 37 mm

paperback (*abbr* pb): *n* a book with covers made of paper, laminated paper or card, but not *boards*.

paperback auction: *n* an *auction* where the *paperback rights* of a book are offered for sale to the highest bidder.

paperback house: *n* a *publisher* of *paperback* books.

paperback original: *n* a book which is published first as a *paperback* and which might be published later as a *hardback*.

paperback rights: *n* the *right* to publish a book as a *paperback* after it has been published as a *hardback*.

paperwork: *n* the routine part of a job involving dealing with correspondence, reports, accounts *etc*.

para: *abbr* of *paragraph*.

parable: *n* a *story* illustrating a moral or spiritual lesson. (Greek: 'proverb'.)

paradox: *n* something that appears to be absurd or even impossible but which is or might be true; a self-contradictory statement. (Greek: 'beside-opinion'.)

paragraph (*abbr* para): *n* a section in a piece of writing indicating a break in sense; starts on a new line, is often indented, and deals with one main idea. (Greek: 'written by the side'.)

parallel plot story: *n* a *story* in which two or more *plots* are developed separately but concurrently; the plots might or might not converge in the course of the story.

paranormal romance: *n* a *subgenre* of *romantic fiction* describing *stories* with elements of the mystical and/or mythological.

paraphrase: *v* to restate something in a way that condenses and clarifies its meaning. (Greek: 'tell in other words'.)

pararhyme: *n* another name for *half-rhyme*.

paratactic style: *n* the placing of clauses and sentences next to each other with no connecting words or phrases, *eg* in the style of Ernest Hemingway (1899–1961). (Greek: 'place side by side'.) The opposite of *hypotactic style*.

parentheses (singular 'parenthesis'): *pl n* round *brackets*. (In *typesetting*, 'brackets' are square brackets thus [ ].)

parody: *n* the application of the distinctive *style* of a work or writer in such a way as to make a subject absurd, incongruous or frivolous. (Greek: 'mock poem'.)

part title: *n* a right-hand *page* with the *title* of a part of a book.

partwork: *n* a substantial *non-fiction* work issued at regular intervals, like a *magazine*, so that you can buy selected and separate *issues* or collect all the issues and keep them in binders to make up a complete reference work.

pass for press: *v* to tell the printer that the *proofs* have been read, the corrections made, and the work is ready to print.

passion play: *n* a *drama* about the crucifixion of Christ; passion plays have been produced every ten years since 1633 in the German village of Oberammergau.

passive voice: *n* the use of passive rather than active *verbs*; 'being done to' rather than 'doing'. See *active voice*.

password: *n* a word known only to the user, which must be typed in to enable access to a computer system or *file*.

paste-up: *n* the *layout* of a *page*, a number of pages, or possibly a whole book, used in planning the relationship and position of *text(1)*, *illustrations, captions etc.*

pastiche: *n* a piece of work made up of imitations and/or bits of other people's published works. (Italian: 'pastry'.)

pastoral: *adj* describing a peaceful romanticised rural life. (Latin: 'to do with shepherds'.)

pathetic fallacy: *n* the transference of human emotions, qualities and traits to inanimate objects.

pathos: *n* feelings of pity, tenderness, sorrow and the like deliberately aroused in *reader(1)* or audience. (Greek: 'suffering'.) See also *bathos*.

pattern poetry: *n* a seventeenth-century forerunner of *concrete poetry*.

payment on acceptance: *n* the writer's dream deal, all too rare nowadays, when an *editor* pays for your work as soon as he accepts it for *publication(1)*.

pb: *abbr* of 'paperback'.

PDF: see *Portable Document Format*.

pe: *abbr* of *printer's error*.

peer review: *n* a *review* of a piece of work by other experts in the same field.

pen name: *n* a name other than your own that you use on your writing; also called *pseudonym*. (Greek: 'false name'.)

penalty clause: *n* a *clause(1)* listing the penalties which will be incurred if you don't meet the terms of your *contract*.

pensée: *n* a single idea concisely expressed. (French: 'thought'.)

pentameter: *n* a line of *poetry* consisting of five metrical *feet*.

perfect binding: *n* a method of binding a book where hot glue is applied to the guillotined backs of the collated *signatures*, *ie* binding by sticking rather than sewing. (A misnomer, as the resulting books tend to fall apart with use.) Also called *adhesive binding, cutback binding, thermoplastic binding*.

performance fee: *n* a fee paid for the right to put on a play or read *poetry* or *prose* to a paying audience.

performing right: *n* the *right* to give a public performance of a *copyright* work.

periodical: *n* a *publication(2)* which appears at stated (usually regular) intervals. Not applied to *newspapers*.

periods of English literature: these are widely accepted as being

450–1066 Anglo-Saxon or Old English
1066–1500 Middle English
1500–1660 Renaissance:

1558–1603 Elizabethan
1603–1625 Jacobean
1625–1649 Caroline
1649–1660 Commonwealth (Puritan Interregnum)

1660–1798 Neo–Classical:

1660–1700 Restoration
1700–1745 Augustan
1745–1798 Age of Sensibility

1798–1832 Romantic
1832–1901 Victorian
1901–1914 Edwardian
1914–   Modern (1910–1936 Georgian)

periphrasis: *n* another term for *circumlocution*. (Greek: 'roundabout speech'.)

Perl: see *Practical Extraction and Reporting Language*.

permission: *n* the *agreement* that must be obtained from the holder of *copyright* to allow the reproduction of passages from a work beyond *fair dealing*.

permit: *n* an official *document* allowing something to be done.

personal experience article: *n* an account of an event, ordeal or process of some kind which has been experienced by the writer.

personality: *n* a public figure.

personality profile: *n* a *profile* of a public figure.

personification: *n* the representation of something not human (*eg* an animal or an inanimate object) as a person. (Latin: 'person-making'.)

Petrarchan sonnet: *n* an Italian *sonnet* named after the poet Petrarch, having 14 lines consisting of an *octave*, *rhyme scheme* abbaabba, followed by a *sestet*, rhyme scheme cdecde.

philology: *n* the study of language. (Greek: 'love of learning and language'.)

phishing: *v* sending scam *e-mails* in the hope of obtaining personal information like bank account details.

phonetics: *n* the study of speech sounds.

photocopy: *n* a photographic reproduction of written or printed *matter*.

photo-feature: *n* a *feature* where the pictures are more important and prominent than the words.

photo-library: *n* a business which stores photographs and leases *reproduction rights;* see also *picture agency*.

photomontage: *n* images from different photographs put together to make a new composite image.

photo-journalism: *n* material (usually news reporting) in which the photographs are more important than the *text(1)*.

photostat (*abbr* stat): *n* a *photocopy*.

photo-story script: *n* a *story* told as a sequence of photographs with *captions* and possibly *balloons*, as distinct from a *picture-story*.

pic (*pl* pix): *n* jargon for 'picture'; commonly used in *journalism*.

pica: *n* a print measurement, one sixth of an inch; the equivalent of 12 point.

pica em: *n* a measure of the width of *type* equivalent to *pica* or 12 point.

picaresque: *adj* a descriptive term applied to humorous or satirical stories about the adventures of a rogue, usually described in great detail, *eg* 'The History of Tom Jones, A Foundling' (1748) by Henry Fielding. (Spanish: 'to do with rogues'.)

pictorial: *adj* like a picture.

picture agency/picture library: *n* a business which stores photographs and/or *illustrations*, leasing *reproduction rights*. Some specialise, others stock a wide range of subjects. See also *photo-library*.

picture book: *n* a book for children, made up of pictures with a short simple *text(1)*, or with pictures only.

picture credit: *n* a *credit* relating to *illustrations*.

picture editor: see under *editor*.

picture fee: *n* 1. a fee paid for the *right* to reproduce a photograph or *illustration* in which the user does not hold the *copyright*. 2. a fee paid by a *publisher* to a writer for the right to reproduce his photograph or *illustration*.

picture library: see *picture agency.*

picture research: *n* the finding of suitable *pictorial* material for reproduction.

picture-script: see *picture-strip.*

picture-story: *n* a *story* told as a sequence of artist-drawn pictures, with *dialogue* shown in *balloons*, and perhaps with supplementary *captions.*

picture-strip: *n* a short sequence of drawings or photographs telling a *story*; also called a *picture-script*; usually applied to *cartoon-strips.*

picturisation book rights: *n* the *right* to publish in book form *cartoons* which have been published in *newspapers.*

piece: *n jargon* for any short piece of writing.

piece rate: *n* a rate of pay per unit of work produced, as distinct from payment by the hour.

piecework: *n* work paid at *piece rate.*

Pindaric ode: *n* a ceremonial *poem*, named after the 5th century Greek lyricist Pindar.

piracy: *n* the illegal copying and/or selling of *copyright* material.

pirate edition: *n* an *edition* of a published book produced without the *permission* of either the *copyright* holder or the legitimate *publisher.*

pitch: 1. *n* the *submission* package you send to a *market(1).* 2. *v* to make an offer of work to a *market(1).*

pix: see *pic.*

plagiarism: *n* the use without *permission* of work in which the *copyright* is held by someone other than the user, whether deliberate or accidental. (Latin: 'kidnapping'.)

plant: *n* in *fiction*, a piece of information fed in unobtrusively, to prepare the *reader(1)*, perhaps subconsciously, for what is to come, thus making the eventual *resolution* convincing and satisfying. See also *foreshadow.*

plate: *n* 1. an engraved piece of metal for printing. 2. a whole-page *illustration.*

platitude: *n* a truth so often stated it has become stale, and is best avoided in writing; *eg* 'You can't have your cake and eat it.' (French: 'flatness'.)

pleonasm: *n* another word for *tautology.* (Greek: 'superfluity'.)

plot: *n* the *storyline*, the scheme of events, the central thread of a *story* with which everything that happens is interwoven.

plot cards: *n* cards on which an *author* files *plots* and plot ideas.

PLR: see *Public Lending Right*.

plug-in: *n software* for extending the capabilities of a *browser*.

pocket edition: *n* an *edition* small enough to be carried in a pocket.

pocket guide: *n* a *guide* in a *format* small enough to be carried easily.

POD: *abbr* of *print on demand*.

podcast: *n* a broadcast made via the *Internet*.

poem: *n* an individual composition, usually in some kind of *metre* and/or *rhyme*. (Greek: 'something created'.)

poesy: *n* a collective term for the art of *poetry*.

poet: *n* the *author* of a *poem*.

poetaster: *n* a bad *poet*.

poetic drama: *n* a play entirely written in *verse*.

poetic licence: *n* the freedom sometimes claimed by *poets* to break rules customarily observed in *prose* writing.

poetry: *n* the art of the *poet*. (Greek: 'creator'.)

poetry group: *n* people who meet regularly to read, discuss and/or write *poetry*.

point: *n* 1. a full stop. 2. a measurement for *type*, approximately 1/72 of an inch.

point of view: see *viewpoint*.

polemic: *n* passionately argumentative writing, usually concerned with religion or politics. (Greek: 'warlike'.)

police procedural: *n* a *category* of *novel* concerned with a police investigation (usually murder). Although primarily an entertainment, it is more authentic in *tone*, shows more social awareness, respects standard police procedures, and involves more *research* than most other forms of *crime fiction*.

polish: *n* the 'finish' you give your work by meticulous attention to detail.

polysyllabic: *adj* describes long words with many *syllables*. (Greek: 'poly' = 'many'.)

pop-up: *n* an *advertisement* that appears in a separate *window* displayed on top of your current *browser* window.

pop-up book: *n* a book in which the illustrated *spreads* spring up when opened, to form three-dimensional pictures by means of multi-layered cut-outs and interlinked pull-tabs.

popular fiction: *n* a term applied to 'light reading', *eg category* or *genre fiction.*

pornography: *n obscene* literature of little or no artistic merit; also applied to obscene art and photography. (Greek: 'writing of whores'.)

port: *n* a socket or similar physical connection allowing the transfer of data between a computer and an external device.

Portable Document Format (abbr. PDF): *n* a type of *file* used for creating and reading electronic books and *documents* on a computer; a product of Adobe Systems.

portal: *n* a *website* allowing links to information and to other websites.

portfolio: *n* a collection of original works.

portion and outline: *n* a sample (usually two or three *chapters*) of a book's contents plus a *synopsis* of the whole book; the usual form in which a *proposal* is submitted to a *publisher.*

portmanteau word: *n* invented by Lewis Carroll, a word formed by combining two words, as in 'slithy', a combination of 'slimy' and 'lithe', from 'Alice Through the Looking Glass'(1871).

portrait: *n* 1. a word picture, a verbal description, usually of a person or *character(1)*. 2. *n* the most usual book *format*, where the depth is greater than the height. See also *landscape.*

post: *v* to display on the *Internet.*

posthumous: *adj* published or printed after the *author's* death.

posting: *n* a message sent to and displayed on, *eg*, a *bulletin board* or an *Internet newsgroup.*

postscript (*abbr* PS): *n* an afterthought added to a finished book or letter.

pot-boiler: *n* a derogatory term applied to a book produced for the sole purpose of earning a living (keeping the domestic pot boiling); often written under *pseudonyms* by well known writers to subsidise more prestigious but less profitable writing, thus protecting their literary reputation.

Practical Extraction and Reporting Language (*abbr* Perl): a scripting language commonly used on the *web.*

précis: *n* an *abridgement* or summary of a longer *text(1)*. (French: 'exactly expressed'.)

preface: *n* an explanatory *introduction* to a work. (Latin: 'speak before'.) See also *foreword*.

prefatory note: *n* an *author's* note to the *reader(1)*, printed at the beginning of a book.

prefix: *n* a word or letters placed before or attached to the beginning of a word, to amplify or change its meaning; *eg* 'Queen Elizabeth', 'mis/inform'.

preliminary letter: see *letter of enquiry*.

prelims: *n* the preliminary *pages* of a book, *ie* the pages before the main *matter*; the *title page*, publishing history, *contents etc*, sometimes numbered with *roman numerals*, for flexibility during *typesetting*.

premise: *n* a brief and concise explanation of subject matter.

premium book: *n* a book offered as an incentive at a very cheap price to members of, *eg*, a *book club*.

prequel: *n* a *story* inspired by the success of a *novel*, film or television series, and written about events that happened before and that led up to the action in the original work; see *eg* Jean Rhys's novel 'The Wide Sargasso Sea' (1966), a prequel to Charlotte Brontë's 'Jane Eyre' (1847). See also *sequel*.

prescribed text: *n* an educational book listed as required reading for a course or exam.

presell: *v* to sell a book before its official *publication date*.

presentation: *n* the manner in which material, *eg* a letter or *manuscript*, is set out.

presentation copy: *n* a copy of a book, perhaps in a special binding or with a special inscription, presented to someone at an official ceremony.

presentation visual: *n* material produced to demonstrate the proposed appearance of a printed work. See also *dummy*, *paste-up*.

press: *n* 1. a publishing and/or printing company. 2. a printing machine. 3. a general term applied to *newspapers*.

press agent: *n* a person who organises publicity.

press copy: *n* a copy of a new book sent to *newspapers* in the hope of generating *reviews*.

press cutting: *n* an item clipped from a *newspaper*.

press cutting agency: *n* an agency which, for a fee and either one-off or on a regular basis, will search through a wide variety of printed *media* to find references to a specified subject or person, and supply *cuttings* of those references.

press officer: *n* a person responsible for a company's *media* publicity.

press proof: *n* the last *proof* to be checked before printing begins.

press release: *n* an announcement intended to be published, 'releasing' information via the *press(3)*.

primary sources: *n research* material that gives original first-hand information, *eg* personal papers, *diaries*, letters *etc*.

primer: *n* a simple basic instruction book.

print media: *pl n newspapers*, *magazines*, books, *journals(1) etc* which are printed in *hard copy*.

print on demand (*abbr* POD): *n* the printing and binding by digital technology of books in small numbers as required.

print run: *n* 1. the total number of copies printed at any one time. 2. the number of copies printed for each separate edition when two or more *editions* are produced simultaneously.

printer's error (*abbr* pe): *n* an error for which the *typesetter*, rather than the *author* or *editor*, is responsible.

printing history: *n* details of a book's printing, such as the original *publication date*, dates of *reprints etc*, usually printed on the *bibliographic page*.

printout: *n* a *hard copy* of a computer *file*.

private detective: *n* a detective who operates under licence but independently of the police, for private clients.

private eye: *n slang* for *private detective*.

private press: *n* a company which prints limited numbers of books, possibly *set* by hand, for sale to collectors.

producer: *n* the person in over-all charge of preparing a programme for radio or television.

production schedule: *n* a written or printed plan, often adjusted and up-dated as production progresses, detailing the various stages of a project and giving the *deadlines* for each stage.

professionalism: *n* the discipline of conducting all business in a professional manner, being businesslike in all dealings with *publishers*, in handling correspondence, in presenting clean reliable *copy*, in meeting *deadlines* etc.

professional journal: *n* a *publication(2)* produced specifically for circulation in a particular profession, *eg* 'The Lancet' (medicine).

professional publishing: *n* the publishing of books about professions like *eg* law and accountancy.

profile: *n* a biographical verbal *sketch*, usually short, published in a *newspaper* or *magazine*; the term is reported to have been used first by 'The New Yorker' in 1925.

program: *n* the universally accepted spelling of 'programme' when related to computing.

promotion: *n* publicity, posters, leaflets, *author* tours, *interviews*, *book signings*, discount incentives *etc* – anything that will generate and boost sales.

proof: *n* a preliminary printing out of *typeset matter* for checking and correction. See *first proof* and *page proof*.

proof correction marks: *n* a standard set of signs and *symbols(1)* commonly used and understood by everyone involved in creating a *publication(2)*, to indicate corrections and alterations to *proofs*. Find them in *eg* 'The Writers' & Artists' Yearbook', or *online*.

proofreader: *n* a person who reads and corrects *proofs*, comparing them with the original *manuscript*.

proofreader's eye: *n* a highly developed ability to spot *printer's errors*.

proofreading: *v* part of the production process, in which the *publisher's proofreaders* and the *author* read *proofs* and mark corrections.

proposal: *n* a summary of an idea for a book, usually put to a *publisher* as an initial query ('Would you be interested in seeing . . . ?'), then, if the response is favourable, as a sales package including a detailed *synopsis* or a *portion and outline* or, if requested, the complete *manuscript*.

prose: *n* writings not in *verse*; the usual form of spoken and written language. (Latin: 'direct'.)

prose poem: *n* a *prose* work that has some of the characteristics of *poetry* such as ornate language and *imagery*.

prosody: *n* the study of the theory and development of poetic forms. (Latin: 'accent of a *syllable*'.)

protagonist: *n* the main *character(1)* usually called the *lead* or *key character*. (Latin: 'first combatant'.)

protocol: *n* a set of rules governing the transfer of data from one computer to another.

proverb: *n* a short pithy saying embodying a general truth; *eg* 'A stitch in time saves nine'.

provincial press: *n* *newspapers* printed in areas outside a country's capital city.

PS: *abbr* of *postscript*.

pseudonym: see *pen name*.

psychological article: *n* an *article* dealing with human behaviour.

psychological novel: *n* a *novel* which focuses on its *characters'(1)* emotional and mental *motivations* and resulting actions, looking at why things happen rather than at how they happen.

public domain, in the: *adj* a term applied to work that has never been protected by *copyright* or work which has become freely available for use by anyone, either because the copyright period has lapsed or by agreement with the copyright holder.

public domain software: *n software* that is not in *copyright* and therefore free for anyone to use; *aka freeware*.

Public Lending Right (PLR): *n* a system of annual monetary reward for writers, based on an estimate of the number of times their works are borrowed from public libraries. The calculation is made from figures supplied by a representative selection of libraries.

publication: *n* 1. the act of publishing. 2. a *magazine, newspaper*, book and suchlike that is published.

publication date: *n* a date fixed by the *publisher* before which a work should not be sold to the public; frequently breached.

publicist: *n* a person who organises publicity.

publicity department: *n* the department in a *publishing house* responsible for promoting and advertising the company's *publications(2)* and activities.

publish: *n* to produce and offer for sale.

published price: *n* the price on the cover and as advertised, at which a *publication(2)* is offered for sale.

publisher: *n* an individual or, collectively, a number of people forming a company, undertaking the creation and selling of published works.

Publishers Association (*abbr* PA): an organisation which represents the interests of publishers in the UK.

publisher's list: see *list*.

publisher's reader: *n* a person employed by a *publisher* to read and evaluate *manuscripts* and to supply summaries and reports, to help the publisher assess their potential as published works; might be a company employee or a *freelance*.

publisher's representative: *n* a salesman who visits book-shops on behalf of a *publisher*, to persuade them to order from the publisher's *list*.

publishing house: *n* a term applied to any sizeable publishing company.

puff: *n* a comment about a book made by an appropriate and well known person and/or *publication(2)*; *eg* 'Couldn't put it down! "Sunday Times"' *etc*, quoted on a book *jacket*. Puffs are not paid for, so are regarded generally as genuine words of praise, recommendation and appreciation.

pull-out: see *fold-out*.

pull-out section: *n* pages of a *periodical* designed to be detached and kept, either as a *booklet* or as part of a series.

pull quote: *n* a *quotation* extracted from an *article* and printed prominently on the *page*.

pulp: 1. *v* to reduce to pulp and make paper from books (usually *paperbacks*) which can't be sold or *remaindered*. 2. *n* cheap *publications(2)* produced on wood-pulp paper which tends to 'yellow' quickly.

pulp fiction: *n* a derogatory term applied to cheaply produced *fiction*, implying that it has no critical value.

pun: *n* a play on words that sound the same but have different meanings; *eg* 'the "write" way to get published'.

punctuation marks: *n* marks included in writing to make sense of the words, helping to clarify their meaning: commas, semi-colons, full stops, question marks, *quotation marks etc*.

Purdue University Online Writing Lab: see *OWL*.

purple patch: *n* a descriptive passage in *prose* or *verse* written in an overblown manner, with extravagant *adverbs*, *adjectives*, contrived *rhythms* and so on, thus appearing incongruous with the rest of the *text(1)*. Originated from Horace, '. . . standing out like a purple patch on white cloth'. ('Ars Poetica', 1st century BC.)

put to bed: *v* to send an *edition* of magazines, *newspapers etc* to the printing presses.

pyrrhic: *n* a metrical *foot(1)* consisting of two short unstressed *syllables*. (Greek: 'war dance'.)

Q

QA: see *query author*.

Q&A: see *Question & Answer*.

quality daily: *n* a *daily newspaper* aimed at the top of the market.

quantity discount: *n* a discount in price given on the purchase of large numbers of a product.

quarterly: *n* a *publication(2)* that appears every three months.

quarto: *n* the size of most modern *hardback* books. (Latin: 'fourth'.)

quatrain: *n* a *stanza* of four lines; usually, the second and fourth lines *rhyme*. (French: 'of four'.)

query: *n* an enquiry from a writer to an *editor* asking if they would be interested in seeing a piece of work; same as *letter of enquiry*.

query author (*abbr* QA): *n* a note asking the *author* to check a particular point in the *text(1)*.

question and answer (*abbr* Q&A): *n* an *interview* or other *piece* in the form of a series of questions and answers.

questionnaire: *n* a written list of questions asking respondents to supply the answers.

quintain: *n* a five-line *stanza* of any *metre* or *rhyme scheme*. (Latin: 'of five'.)

quintet: *n* another name for *quintain*. (Latin: 'little fifth'.)

quod vide (*abbr* qv): *n* Latin for 'which see', indicating a *cross-reference*.

quotation (*abbr* quote): *n* an extract from a literary work, used as a verbal *illustration*, reinforcement, reference or *allusion*.

quotation mark (*abbr* quote): *n* a *punctuation mark*, usually a single or double inverted comma, before and after quoted *matter*.

quote: *n* 1. see *quotation*. 2. see *quotation mark*. 3. an estimation of cost.

qv: see *quod vide*.

'qwerty' keyboard: *n* the standard keyboard – these are the left-hand letters of the top row of letter keys.

R

rabelaisian writing: *n* humorous, exuberant, bawdy writing; derives from the 16th century French writer Rabelais.

radio rights: *n* the *right* to adapt and broadcast a work on radio.

ragged right: same as *unjustified*.

RAM: see *random access memory*.

random access memory (*abbr* RAM): *n* the primary working memory in a computer, which can be accessed for storing and modifying data.

range: *v* an instruction to the *typesetter* to align *matter* to right or left as indicated.

rare book: *n* a modern book (less than 75 years old), out of print and difficult to find.

raster graphics: *n* graphics in which the images are built up in lines across the *page* or screen.

read only memory (*abbr* ROM): *n* a computer system which allows *text(1)* to be read but not edited.

read-through: *n* the reading aloud of a *script(1)* by actors, without performance.

readability: *n* the quality of being easy and/or enjoyable to read.

reader: *n* 1. a person who reads printed material. 2. an expert consultant, a reviewer of *manuscripts*. See also *publisher's reader, proofreader*.

reader identification: *n* the art of enabling the *reader(1)* to identify with a *character(1)*, to imagine they are the character, living the story and taking part in the action.

reader profile: *n* the perceived average *reader(1)* of a *publication(2)*, assessed in terms of age range, social status, spending power, educational level and leisure interests.

reader's report: *n* a written summary of and opinion on the worth of a submitted *manuscript*. See *publisher's reader*.

reader's letter: *n* correspondence from a *reader(1)* published in a *newspaper* or *magazine*; sometimes paid for in money or prizes.

readership: *n* a collective term applied to the people who regularly read a particular *publication(2)*.

reading copy: *n* 1. a copy of a book supplied to an appropriate person, such as a school-teacher, in the hope of generating a large order; see *inspection copy*. 2. an *advance copy*, possibly not yet up to the final published standards. 3. in book-collecting, a copy in such poor condition it has no value other than for its content.

reading fee: *n* a fee paid to an *agent*, *magazine* or *publisher* to read a submitted *manuscript*. Usually refundable in the event of *acceptance* and *publication(1)*. (Note that reputable companies do not normally charge such a fee.)

ream: *n* 500 sheets of paper.

rebus: *n* a *story* or puzzle in which words or names (or parts of these) are represented by pictures. Readers of *detective fiction* will recognise the word as the name of the main *character(1)*, Detective-Inspector Rebus, in a series of Edinburgh-set *novels* by Scottish writer Ian Rankin (1960–).

recording rights: *n* the *right* to make a record of a piece of music, a *poem*, or a reading of a book.

recto page: *n* the right-hand *page* of an open book. (Latin: 'right'.)

red herring: *n* a false clue meant to mislead, usually in *detective fiction*. Originated in England, probably in the 17th century, where anti-foxhunt activists would drag smoked – thus red – herrings across the fox's track to throw the dogs off the scent.

reference book: *n* an information book in which you can look things up, like a dictionary or *encyclopaedia*.

reference library: *n* a library where the books or *documents* cannot be borrowed but can only be read within the premises.

reference mark: *n* a sign used in a *text(1)* to refer to *footnotes*, in the order * † ‡ § ¶.

reference publisher: *n* a *publisher* who publishes *reference books*.

refrain: *n* words or lines repeated in the course of a *poem* or song. (Latin: 'to break'.)

regency romance: *n* a *subgenre* of *romantic fiction*, describing *stories* set in the British Regency period (1811–20).

regional magazine: *n* a *magazine* produced in a particular region of the country, reflecting the interests of the people of that region.

regional newspaper: *n* a *newspaper* publishing news of personalities and events within a well defined region, covering a wider area than a *local newspaper* but not usually concerned with national news other than how that news might affect its own *readership*.

regional novel: *n* a *novel* featuring the *setting(2)*, customs and speech of a particular locality as major influences and not merely as *local colour*; *eg* the 'Wessex' novels of Thomas Hardy (1840–1928).

regular feature: *n* a *feature* appearing at regular intervals in a *newspaper* or *magazine, eg* an *agony column*.

rehash: *n* previously published material used in a different form, perhaps with new *illustrations* and a new *format*.

reissue: *n* an *out-of-print publication(2)* resurrected and published again either by the original *publisher* or by another.

rejection fee: *n* a fee paid to a *freelance* who has been asked to produce material which is then discarded. See also *kill fee*.

rejection slip: *n* a printed slip, usually small and impersonal, sent with a rejected *unsolicited manuscript* to express 'the editor's regrets' that the material is not wanted.

relevance: see *suitability*.

religious press: *n* a *publishing house* which specialises in religious books.

religious writing: *n* books, *features, stories* and other material dealing with religious topics, intended for *publication(1)* by *publishers, newspapers* and *magazines* concerned with religious matters.

remainders: *n* leftover and unsaleable stock offered by *publishers* at 'scrap' value to specialist dealers ('morticians') who then resell through discount shops.

repartee: *n* a swift reply, often slightly insulting. (French: 'reply swiftly'.)

report: *n* a *document* giving an exact description of something that happened.

reportage: *n* 1. a *style* of writing which reports events without offering opinion or interpretation. 2. *photo-journalism* which gives information mainly through photographic images.

reporter: *n* a person employed (usually by a *newspaper*) to report news as early as possible.

reporting time: *n* American for *response time*.

reprint: *n* a second or further printing without alteration.

reprint house: *n* a *publishing house* specialising in republishing *out of print titles*.

reprint rights: *n* the *right* to republish a book, either in its original form or in a different *format* or version after first *publication(1)*.

reproduction fee: *n* a fee paid to a *copyright* owner for *permission* to reproduce a *text(1)* or picture.

reproduction rights: *n* the *right* to reproduce *copyright* material in a specified form.

research: *n* the systematic investigation of a subject.

researcher: *n* a person who carries out *research*, either as an employee of a *publishing house* or on a *freelance* basis.

reserve: *n* funds held back from the *author's royalty* against the *publisher's* estimate of books that might be returned unsold by *booksellers*.

residual rights: *n* 1. *rights* not specifically defined in a *contract*. 2. *rights* licensed to a *publisher* but remaining unexploited during the licence period.

resolution: *n* the conclusion of a *story*: the unmasking of the murderer, the coming together of the lovers, the *twist in the tail etc*; the end result of all the action.

resonance: *n* the enduring impact of a *story*.

response time: *n* the time taken to assess and respond to an *unsolicited manuscript*.

rest of the world (*abbr* RoW): *n* territory outside any specified area.

résumé: *n* a summary or *synopsis*. In the USA, the term has the same meaning as the UK *curriculum vitae*. (French: 'summary'.)

retainer: *n* a fee paid by a *publisher* to a *freelance* to secure their continuing availability to produce material for that publisher.

retouch: *v* to improve photographs, transparencies or digital photo-files to remove blemishes and/or obtain better colour reproduction.

returns: *n* books or *magazines* ordered by *booksellers* or newsagents, not sold, and subsequently returned to source for credit.

revenge tragedy: *n* a type of *tragedy* focusing on the *protagonist's* pursuit of vengeance against those he perceives to have wronged him; *eg* Shakespeare's 'Hamlet' (*c* 1600) and John Webster's 'The Duchess of Malfi' (1623).

reversal: *n* an emotional turnabout by a *character(1)* resulting from an experience or from an internal realisation.

reverse indent: see *hanging indent*.

reversion clause: *n* a *clause* in a *contract* providing that if a book goes *out of print* or its *publisher* ceases trading the *author* (or the author's *agent*) can ask for the return of agreed *rights* other than those already sub-leased to other parties.

review: *n* a *critique* recommending (or not) a work to potential purchasers.

review article: *n* a long *review* in which the subject of a book is discussed rather than the book itself.

review copy: *n* a free copy sent by a *publisher* before *publication(1)* to an individual or *publication(2)* in the hope of generating a favourable *review*.

review list: *n* a list of individuals and/or *periodicals* where a *publisher* proposes to send *review copies*.

review slip: *n* a brief note sent with each *review copy* giving information such as price and *publication date*.

revision: *n* the examination and correction of a work by its *author* before preparation of a *fair copy*.

revue: *n* a theatrical entertainment made up of *sketches(2)*, jokes, songs and dances.

re-write: 1. *v* to write unpublished work again, perhaps acting on an *editor's* suggestions. 2. *n* a re-written version.

rhetoric: *n* the art of speaking effectively, to persuade an audience. (Greek: 'rhetor' = 'public speaker'.)

rhetorical question: *n* a question asked to emphasise a point rather than to seek an answer, the answer being taken for granted.

rhyme: *n* the repetition of the same or similar sounds. (Greek: 'rhythm'.)

rhyme royal: *n* a type of *poetry* whose *stanzas* have seven ten-*syllable* lines in *iambic pentameter*, *rhyme scheme* ababbcc.

rhyme scheme: *n* the pattern of *rhymes* in a *stanza* or section of *verse*, usually shown as an alphabetic code, *eg* ababcdcd *etc*.

rhythm: *n* variations in levels of stress in language or in the pacing of a *story* – the 'beat'. (Greek: 'flowing'.)

rich text format (*abbr* RTF): *n* a *text(1)* *file format* which includes commands that control the *page*, *font*, *type* and formatting.

rider: *n* an additional *clause* in a *contract*.

right: *n* a legal entitlement.

right-hand page: *n* the *page* on the right of a *double-page spread*, always with an odd page number; also called *recto page*.

right justification: *n* the *alignment* of the right-hand edge of the *text(1)*.

rights: *n* those parts of an *author's copyright* which he leases to a *publisher* as specified in a *contract*.

rights manager: *n* a person in charge of the *rights* department of a company.

rising rhythm: *n* refers to *iambic* and *anapaestic metres* in which the stress pattern rises (ti-tum) rather than falls (tum-ti).

river: *n* an accidental formation of word spaces into an undesirable 'stream' of white space running through a *text(1)*.

role: *n* the function of a *character(1)*, who he is, what he does, why he does it *etc.*

role-building: *v* the creating and building up of a fictional *character(1)* by giving them a complete *characterisation* and history before writing a *story*, even though only a small amount of this information will be given in the story, so keeping personality, *motivation* and actions (the character's *role*) consistent and credible.

ROM: see *read only memory*.

roman à clef: *n* a *novel* in which the *reader(1)* is given clues (keys) designed to enable the identification of real people and/or events under the fictional surface. (French: 'novel with a key'.)

roman fleuve: *n* a series of *novels*, each complete in itself, following the fortunes of the same *characters(1)*; a famous example is 'A la Recherche du Temps Perdu' by Marcel Proust (1871–1922). (French: 'novel-river'.)

Roman numerals/roman figures: *n* numbers shown as, *eg*, iii, iv, x, or II, IV, X *etc.*

Roman type: *n* upright *type*, the most commonly used in printed *texts(1)*.

romantic comedy: *n* a *subgenre* of *romantic fiction*, in which *stories* are upbeat with humour playing a large part.

romantic fiction: *n* love stories.

romantic historical: *n* a *subgenre* of *romantic fiction* in which stories are set in the past.

romantic poets: *n* a term describing the English poets who wrote during the Romantic Period (1798–1832); included Blake, Wordsworth, Coleridge, Southey, Byron, Shelley and Keats.

romantic suspense: *n* a *subgenre* of *romantic fiction* which blends elements of *romance, suspense* and *mystery*.

rondeau: *n* a lyrical *poem* of French origin consisting of three *stanzas* and featuring a *refrain* which picks up the first word or phrase of the poem. (French: 'round'.) The full lines, none of which are repeated, may be of any length and metre. *Rhyme scheme* aabba,aabR, aabbaR (R representing 'refrain'). *Eg*

> I dropped my ring; watched ripples crease a line
> of iced black water, give the only sign
> of movement in the stillness of this cave.
> I stooped, as if I thought that I could save
> my ring from slipping through earth's fissured spine.
>
> In truth, my clumsiness was by design.
> The subterranean channels of the mine
> were tomb black, hushed and older than the grave.
>   I dropped my ring.
>
> When I am long gone, then my ring will shine,
> reborn and new discovered, crystalline
> reminder I once trod this timeless wave
> whose tide change grips us all. For this I gave
> your gift, full circle, love and soul entwined.
>   I dropped my ring.
> (© Alison Chisholm, 'Silver Ring Rondeau'.)

rondel: *n* a medieval French *verse* form consisting of fourteen lines divided into three *stanzas*, repeating the first and second lines as lines seven and eight and again as lines thirteen and fourteen; *rhyme scheme* either ABba,abAB,abbaAB, or ABab,BAAB,ababAB. *Eg* (first rhyme scheme)

> The people thought their rescuers would come.
> This ship was safer than the frozen sea,
> so passengers ignored the Captain's plea.
> Unsinkable, this ship would not succumb.
>
> Ripped open by the ice, she still had some
> faint hope of floating. They would soon be free,
> the people thought. Their rescuers would come.
> This ship was safer than the frozen sea.
>
> Iced inrush jarred her equilibrium
> until she foundered. Then too late to flee

> her passengers screamed their last agony,
> fell silent as a black flood struck them dumb.
> The people thought their rescuers would come –
> this ship was safer than the frozen sea.
> (© Alison Chisholm, '14th April, 1912'.)

rough: *n* an elementary preliminary *outline* to show how an idea will be approached.

rough draft: *n* a first or early stage of a work, intended for much subsequent *revision*, re-writing and possibly re-structuring.

round-up article: *n* an *article* in which a number of people with something in common (occupation, hobby, status, age group, characteristics *etc*) respond to the same question(s) or give an opinion on the same topic; also called a *survey article*.

router: *n* a device that manages the data traffic between computers and other devices.

RoW: *n abbr* of 'rest of the world', *ie* anywhere outside a specified geographic area.

royalty: *n* a payment, usually a percentage of either the *list price* or the *net receipts* of a book payable to the *author* under the terms of a *contract* after any *advance* has been recovered; how much is paid depends on the number of books sold. Usually paid either yearly or half-yearly.

royalty split: *n* the division of a *royalty* between two or more *authors* or between author and *illustrator*.

royalty statement: *n* a printed *document* showing how much *royalty* is due to be paid to an *author* by a *publisher*.

royalty-free copy: *n* a book on which no royalty payment is due to the *author*; covers *complimentary copies* given to the author under the terms of the *contract*, books sent out without charge for *review* or publicity purposes, and books returned from bookshops or wholesalers.

RTF: see *rich text format*.

.rtf: *n* an extension for an *RTF* file.

rubai: *n* an Arabic *quatrain* form, written in *iambic pentameter*, with a *rhyme* pattern of aaxa, bbxb, ccxc and so on; *eg* Edward Fitzgerald's translation of 'The Rubaiyat of Omar Khayyam' (4th revised edition 1879):

> The moving finger writes: and having writ,
> Moves on: nor all your piety nor wit

Shall lure it back to cancel half a line,
Nor all your tears wash out a word of it.

rubric: *n* a set of instructions or rules like *eg* those at the beginning of an examination paper.

rule: *n* 1. a printed line of specified thickness. 2. a condition of entry in a competition.

run: see *print run*.

run-around: *n* a term for *text(1)* fitted around an *illustration* or design element which occupies only part of the full text area.

run back: *v* to take printed *matter* back to the preceding line(s) to compensate for an alteration that would otherwise leave *unoccupied* space.

rune: *n* one of twenty-four letters carved on wood or stone by the Anglo-Saxons; the oldest kind of writing in Britain. (Old Norse: 'magical sign'.)

run-in heading: *n* a heading *set* in the same line as the opening of the *text(1)* that follows it.

run on/follow on: 1. *v* an instruction to the *typesetter* to make the *text(1)* read straight on without a *paragraph* break. 2. *adj* describing a *chapter* that begins on the same page on which the previous chapter ends, rather than starting on a fresh page. 3. *n* copies of a book printed in addition to the number required to cover the fixed costs.

running cost: *n* the current cost of printing and binding.

running foot: *n* a line of print at the foot of each *text(1)* *page*.

running heads/running headlines: *n* *headlines* at the top of *pages*, above the *text(1)* area, which repeat the book *title(1)* on each page, or perhaps repeat the book title on all the *verso* or *recto* pages with the *chapter titles*, or possibly the *author's* name, on the facing pages.

running order: *n* 1. the order of events in a production. 2. a list of the contents of a printed work, a guide to the printer in his *imposition*.

rush job: *n* a job that has to be done quickly.

S

saddle-stitching: *n* a method of stitching or stapling a *booklet* or *magazine* through the back *centre fold*.

sae: see *stamped addressed envelope*.

sag: *n* loss of *tension* or *suspense*, usually caused by a patch of slack writing, *wordiness*, or the introduction of an irrelevance, *eg* a superfluous incident or *character(1)*.

saga: *n* originally a *story* about the exploits of heroes, the term is now applied to any lengthy story about a family's triumphs and tragedies, usually covering several generations. (Old Norse: 'proverb'.)

samizdat: *n* publishing by private individuals or by a group in a country where the state has a monopoly and where publishing is censored. (Russian: 'do-it-yourself publishing'.)

sans: see *sans serif font*.

sans serif font: *n* a *font* without *serifs*; often called simply *sans*.

Sapphic ode: *n* a type of *ode* named after the female *poet* Sappho (7th century BC), consisting of three-line *stanzas* mixing *dactyls*, *spondees* and *trochees*. Mainly found in experimental work by Tennyson (1809–92) and Swinburne (1837–1909).

sarcasm: *n* an extreme form of *irony* intended to wound. (Greek: 'speak bitterly'.)

sase: see *stamped addressed envelope*.

satire: *n* the art of diminishing a subject by poking fun at it, sometimes gently but often with ridicule or contempt. (Latin: 'medley'.)

sc: *abbr* of *small capitals*.

scamp: *n* a very rough *layout* of *text(1)* and *illustrations*.

scanning: *n* a process by which printed *text(1)* and photographs are read by computer scanner and converted into usable data.

scansion: *n* the study and analysis of *metre*. (Latin: 'measuring'.)

scatology: *n* obscene literature closely related to *pornography*; derives from the study of fossil excrement. (Greek: 'dung knowledge'.)

scatter proof: *n* a sheet showing several *illustrations* in random order.

scenario: *n* 1. a summary of a film or play, sketching out *plot* and *characters(1)*. 2. the way in which a situation is likely to develop.

scene: *n* 1. a sub-division of an *act*. 2. a unit of action and time in a *story*. (Latin: 'stage'.)

scholarly press: *n* a company that publishes books intended for students who already have some knowledge of a subject.

school book: *n* an educational book for use in schools.

school edition: *n* an *edition* of a book made specifically for sale to schools.

science fiction (*abbr* 'SF', not 'sci-fi'**)**: *n* a *genre* dealing with the possibilities suggested by scientific and technological developments as they might affect the human race, with imaginative *stories* set on earth in the future, on other planets, or in space.

scientific, technical and medical publishing (*abbr* STM**)**: *n* publishing focused on books in these specific fields.

scissors-and-paste job: *n* a contemptuous term applied to an unimaginative piece of work formed by metaphorically (and sometimes literally) cutting out and rearranging bits of other people's thought, *research* and writing, with little evidence of the writer's own original thought, feeling or opinion. See also *rehash*.

scoop: *n* an important news story which a *reporter* is first to find.

score: *n* written or printed music.

scout: *n* a person who seeks out material and/or writers on behalf of a *publisher* or *producer*.

screamer: *n* publishing jargon for an exclamation mark.

screenplay: *n* a film *script(1)* that includes cinematic information, *eg* camera movements, as well as *dialogue*.

screenwriting: *v* writing for film and television.

script: *n* 1. a *text(1)* for acting or broadcasting. 2. *abbr* of *manuscript* or *typescript*.

scriptwriter: *n* a writer who creates or adapts material to make a *script(1)*.

scroll: *v* to move *text(1)* up and down a computer screen.

search and replace: *n* a *word processing* facility that lets you find words or combinations of *characters(2)* and change them all at once with one command; also called *find and replace*.

search engine: *n* an electronic *catalogue* that can store and find an infinite number of *website* addresses.

seasonal material: *n* material designed to be published or performed at a specific time of the year, *eg* Christmas, Easter, Hallowe'en *etc*.

second serial rights: *n* the *right* to publish material in the same or another medium after first *publication(1)*.

secondary source: *n* a source of *research* such as other people's research, books, *articles*, reports *etc*, as distinct from a *primary source*.

section: see *signature*.

section mark: *n* the mark § used as a reference, especially to a *footnote*.

secure website: *n* a *website* that encrypts messages between the visitor and the site to prevent *hacking(2)* or eavesdropping.

see copy: *v* an instruction to the *typesetter* to look at the original *manuscript* to see how the *setting(1)* should be done.

self-cover: *n* a cover made from the same paper and printed at the same time as the leaves of the book it covers.

self criticism: *n* the art of looking critically and dispassionately at your own work, to discern, assess and correct its faults and weaknesses.

self-help article: *n* an *article* that guides, assists and encourages people in coping with their own problems.

self-help book: *n* a book which does the same as a *self-help article* in more depth and at greater length.

self-publishing: *n* a venture in which you publish your book at your own expense, arranging (or doing yourself) all aspects and processes of *publication(1)* from editing to selling. See *vanity publishing*.

semantics: *n* the study of the meaning of words. A plural noun treated as singular. (Greek: 'significant'.)

semi-bold: *n* a *typeface* between standard and *bold*.

semi-colon: *n* a *symbol*; signifying a pause longer than a comma but not final like a full stop. Useful in linking elements in a sentence, but over-use can make *text(1)* look clumsy.

senses: see *five senses*.

sensory information: *n* information that appeals to the *reader(1)'s* senses through description of touch, smell, sound, sight and taste.

sensuous description: *n* similar to *sensory information*.

septet: *n* a seven-line *stanza*.

sequel: *n* a *story* in which the same *characters(1)*, or their descendants, continue the action of an earlier story. See also *prequel*.

serenade: *n* a song or song-like *poem* intended to express feelings towards a loved one while lulling them to sleep. (Italian: 'evening'.)

serial: *n* a *story* divided into parts which are published in sequence in consecutive *issues* of a *periodical*.

serial port: *n* a connector linking a computer to a *modem*.

serial rights: *n rights* covering material sold to *magazines* and *newspapers*; does not necessarily mean that the material will be printed in instalments. See *FBSR*.

serialisation rights: *n* the *right* granted to a *periodical* to reproduce a work in parts spread over several consecutive *issues*.

series: *n* a work published in instalments. Usually applied to a sequence of *stories*, *articles* or books having some basic element in common but each being complete in itself.

serif: *n* a small decorative *tag(2)* added to some *fonts*.

sermon: *n* a discourse on a moral or religious subject. (Latin: 'talk'.)

server: *n* a computer with a large storage capacity which is permanently connected to the *Internet*.

service article: *n* an *article* describing, evaluating and comparing products and services, and possibly also advising consumers about them.

service provider: see *Internet service provider*.

sestet: *n* a group of six lines forming the second part of a *sonnet*. (Italian: 'sixth'.)

sestina: *n* an elaborate *verse* form, Provençal in origin, with six *stanzas* each of six lines of *pentameter*. See *eg* Ezra Pound's 'Sestina in Altaforte' (1909). (Italian: 'little sixth'.)

set: *abbr* of *typeset*.

setting: 1. *v* see *typesetting*. 2. *n* the *location* or *background* of a story.

sexual tension: *n* a vital component of *romantic fiction*; created by a situation where the *hero* and *heroine* are sexually attracted to each other but are unable to act on that attraction.

sf: *abbr* of *science fiction*.

shaggy dog story: *n* a joke in which the lead-up to the (often weak) punch-line is long and full of unnecessary detail.

Shakespearian sonnet: *n* an English development from the *Petrarchan* or Italian sonnet, having a *rhyme scheme* of ababcdcdefefgg. Also called *English sonnet*.

shamus: *n* old American *slang* for a *private detective*.

shape: *n* the *form* or *structure* of a work.

shape poetry: *n poetry* in which the words are formed into the shape of the *poem's* subject by adapting the *typography*; *eg* a poem about wine *set* in the shape of a wine-glass. See also *calligramme, concrete poetry*.

shareware: *n software* you may sample freely, but for which you might be expected to pay a fee to the writer if you keep it.

shelf life: *n* the projected time during which a *publication(2)* will sell.

shibboleth: *n* a word or *catch-phrase* adopted by a person or group and regarded by them as particularly significant. (Hebrew: 'stream'.)

short feature: *n* a *feature article* considerably shorter than other features in a *publication(2)* but longer than a *filler*; usually about 400–900 words.

short message service (*abbr* SMS): *n* a service which lets you send short *text(2)* messages by *eg* mobile phones and pagers.

short run: *n* a small *print run*, usually of a specialist *publication(2)* but sometimes produced to test sales potential before a longer run is printed.

short story: *n* a piece of *fiction*, usually between 1,000 and 8,000 words.

short-short story: *n* a very short piece of *fiction*, of fewer than 1,000 words.

shoulder note: *n* a note printed in the *margin* at the level of the first line of *type*.

shout line: *n* a prominent line of *text(1)* on a *magazine* cover drawing attention to an item featured inside.

shovelware: *n* content from a medium like a book or *newspaper* 'shovelled up' and dumped into a *web page*.

show, don't tell: *v* a much advocated *technique* in *fiction* writing in which the *author* presents the *characters'(1)* speech and actions with little or no *exposition*, and leaves it to the *reader(1)* to interpret their *motives* and intentions.

sibilant: *n* a hissing consonant sound like 's' and 'z'.

sic: *adv*; a Latin word meaning 'thus' or 'so'; indicates that what is shown does reproduce the original although it might appear to be incorrect.

sick verse: *n* 'humorous' *verse* which relies for effect on flippant references to cruelty, death, affliction *etc*; see *eg* 'Isabella' (1820) by John Keats.

sidebar: *n* a short *feature* accompanying a news *story* or an *article*, enlarging on some aspect of the *piece*. Usually boxed or *set* in a different *typeface* or otherwise distinguished from the main *text(1)*.

side-head: *n* a heading *ranged* (usually left) above the *text(1)*.

side note: *n* a note printed in the *margin* at the side of the *text(1)*.

sight unseen: *adj* describing a book accepted by a publisher at a very early stage of writing, possibly before a word has been written. Almost invariably the book is by or about a celebrity or some other well known person, thus guaranteeing high sales.

signature (*abbr* sig): *n* the traditional name for a *section*. 1. a complete printed sheet folded, usually, into 16 or 32 *pages*. 2. a mark printed at the bottom of the first page of such a section, to ensure that the sections are collated in the correct order; might be a letter or *numeral*, or sometimes the initials of the book *title(1)* plus a numeral.

signing-session: *n* an organised visit to a bookshop by an *author* to sign copies of his or her book as they are bought.

simile: *n* a *figure of speech* making a comparison between two different things, indicated by the words 'like' or 'as'. *Eg* 'her hair shone like gold', 'his hands were as hard as iron'. (Latin: 'like'.)

simulcast: *n* a programme broadcast at the same time on radio and television, on television and the *Internet*, *etc*.

simultaneous submission: *n* the same material sent to more than one *market(1)* at a time.

single line spacing: *n* with no white lines between lines of *text(1)*.

single quotation marks/single quotes: *n* printed signs ' ' around a piece of *text(1)* to show that something is quoted.

sit-com: *n abbr* of *situation comedy*.

sitemap: *n* a plan of a *website*.

situation comedy (*abbr* sit-com): *n* a humorous play or serial for radio or television.

sketch: *n* 1. a rough outline or drawing. 2. a short theatrical piece, usually comedic.

skyscraper ad: *n* an *advertisement* that runs vertically down the side of a *web page*.

slander: *n* a spoken statement which is untrue and which damages or threatens to damage someone's reputation.

slang: *n* informal, sometimes racy, colloquial language. (Norwegian: 'offensive language'.)

slant: *n* a particular way of looking at things. See *angle*.

slapstick: *n* broad 'knockabout' *comedy*.

slash: *n* an oblique stroke /; also called a *solidus*.

slice of life: *n* a depiction of life 'as it is', from which *readers(1)* or viewers are meant to draw their own meanings without comment or explanation from the *author*.

slicks (US): *n* glossy *magazines*.

sliding royalty: *n* a *royalty* where the percentage increases with the number of books sold.

slip case: *n* a case or box to hold books, with one side open to show the *spine(s)*.

slogan: *n* a *catch-phrase*, an idea expressed in a few words.

slush pile: *n* a derogatory term applied to the unsolicited, usually unwanted, *manuscripts* that accumulate in an editorial office; so called because of the high proportion of sentimentally *romantic fiction* received in this way.

small cap: see *small capital*.

small capital (*abbrs* small cap, sc): *n* a *capital letter* smaller than standard size, usually the height of the *lower case* x of any particular *font*.

small press: *n* a small business, often a one-person operation, producing *publications(2)* of variable quality ranging from duplicated *pamphlets* to bound books. Usually financed by enthusiasts and relying for survival on subscriptions and/or grants; seldom profitable, they often offer the first step in *publication(1)* for new writers, especially *poets*.

smart quotes: *n* a feature in a *typesetting program* which can automatically convert straight inverted commas into *quotation marks*.

smiley: see *emoticon*.

SMS: see *Short Message Service*.

snail mail: *n slang* for normal postal services, as distinct from electronic mail.

soap/soap opera: *n* originally, radio *drama* sponsored by soap companies as a vehicle for advertising their products. Now applied to serial *dramas*, whether on commercial channels or not.

soap opera: see *soap*.

social issue article: *n* an *article* dealing with issues of concern to society, from topics of widespread interest to local and community matters.

social network: *n* a means of interacting and community building *online*; see *eg Facebook, Myspace* and *Twitter*.

social-problem novel: see *sociological novel*.

Society of Authors, The: *n* a professional society for published authors, and a source of advice and information for all writers; see www.societyofauthors.org.

sociological novel: *n* a *genre* of *novel* which emphasises the influences and effects of social and economic conditions on the lives of its *characters(1)*. Often a vehicle, implicit or explicit, for urging social reform; see *eg* Charles Kingsley's 'Alton Locke' (1850) which explores the conditions of sweat-shop workers in the clothing industry. Also called a social-problem novel.

softback: same as *paperback*.

soft copy: *n* material stored on *eg disk* or computer memory, not on paper.

softcover: see *paperback*.

software: *n* computer *programs* that govern what the *hardware* can do.

solecism: *n* in literature, a grammatical or lexical error betraying the perpetrator's ignorance. (Greek: 'using incorrect syntax'.)

solidus: *n* an oblique stroke /.

soliloquy: *n* a dramatic convention allowing a *character(1)* in a play to speak directly to the audience. See *eg* 'To be or not to be, that is the question' from Shakespeare's 'Hamlet' (1600). (Latin: 'to speak alone'.) See also *monologue*.

sonnet: *n* a *poem* consisting of fourteen lines of *iambic pentameter* of varying *rhyme schemes*; see *Petrarchan sonnet*, *Shakespearian sonnet* and *Spenserian sonnet*. (Italian: 'little sound'.)

sound poetry: *n* dating from the early 20th century, a type of *poetry* meant for performance. Usually has no logical *structure* or meaning, but concentrates on sound alone; *eg*, repetition of a word or words many times in various tones, pitches and rhythms; an oral equivalent of *concrete poetry*. See *eg* the work of Dame Edith Sitwell (1887–1964).

source: *n* a work from which an *author* has taken ideas, images, or even a complete *story*.

source list: *n* a list of people interviewed and reference works consulted in compiling a work; used by *fact checkers* to verify information in an *article*.

spam: *n* uninvited and unwanted *e-mail*.

special interest magazine: *n* a *magazine* catering exclusively for a particular and often narrow field of interest, *eg* 'The Woodworker', 'Practical Photography'.

specification: *n* the specific and detailed design instructions for a *publication(2)*, setting out *format*, *extent*, *typefaces* and sizes, quality of paper and binding *etc*.

specimen chapter: *n* a single *chapter* which will eventually form part of a complete work, supplied as part of a *portion and outline*.

speech tag: *n* a descriptive *verb* used to enrich *characterisation* by showing how a *character(1)* talks, both in terms of the words used and the manner in which they are said; *eg*, '"Shut up!" she spat.'

spell-check: *n* a computer *program* that automatically checks *text(1)* against an internal dictionary.

Spenserian sonnet: *n* a *sonnet* form created by Edmund Spenser (*c* 1552–99), consisting of three *quatrains* and a *couplet*, *rhyme scheme* ababcdcdefefgg.

Spenserian stanza: *n* a form invented by Edmund Spenser for his work 'The Faerie Queen' (1590); consists of eight lines of *iambic pentameter* followed by one of *iambic hexameter*, with the *rhyme scheme* ababbcbcc; a form much borrowed by some of the *romantic poets*.

spin-off: *n* a product generated by the success of a book, play, film or television series: *eg*, 'book of the film', stories featuring minor *characters(1)*, *character merchandising*, toys, games *etc*.

spine: *n* the back edge of a book.

spine lettering: *n* *title(1)*, *author's* name, *publisher's* *colophon(1) etc* printed on a book's *spine* and sometimes also printed in the same position on the *jacket*.

split infinitive: *n* the insertion of a qualifying word into the infinitive of a *verb* instead of before or after it; *eg*, 'To boldly go' instead of the grammatically correct 'To go boldly'. Generally modern usage accepts that it is better to split an infinitive than to put the qualifying word in an awkward or ambiguous position.

split screen: *n* the displaying of more than one image or *text(1)* at the same time on a single screen divided in two.

spondee: *n* a metrical *foot* consisting of two long *syllables* or two strong stresses.

sponsored book: *n* a book subsidised by a commercial, national or government organisation, or possibly by an individual, for publicity and goodwill; often produced by a regular *publishing house*, but with a proportion of the costs met by the sponsor, who might also share the profits.

spoonerism: *n* the transposition of the initial consonants of two words, resulting in a different, possibly nonsensical, meaning; *eg*, 'a half-formed wish' becomes a 'half-warmed fish'. Named after Oxford Don, the Reverend W. A. Spooner (1844–1930).

spread: see *double spread*.

spreadsheet: *n* a computer *program* in which data, formatted in rows and columns, can be viewed on a screen and manipulated to make calculations and projections *etc*.

sprung rhythm: *n* a term invented by the *poet* Gerard Manley Hopkins (1844–89) to explain his own highly complicated *style* and metric system; see the preface to the 1918 edition of his 'Poems'.

squib: *n* a small piece of writing intended to annoy or to express irritation.

square brackets: *n symbols(1)* [ ] used in writing and printing to indicate the insertion of *matter*.

stab-stitching: *v* stitching by wire through the back *margin* of a *magazine* or *booklet*; see also *saddle-stitching*.

stab point: see *bullet*.

stable: *n* 1. a group of writers whose work is regularly commissioned and published by a particular *magazine* or *publishing house* although they are not on its staff. 2. a group of publishing enterprises under the same management or ownership.

staff writer (US: staffer): *n* a writer employed and salaried by a *publisher*, as distinct from a *freelance*.

staffer: see *staff writer*.

stage directions: *n* advice and instructions about the

necessary gestures and movements of actors in a play, sometimes written into the *script(1)*.

stamped addressed envelope (*abbr* sae): *n* an envelope addressed back to the sender, large enough and bearing adequate postage stamps or sent with *IRCs* for the return of submitted material or for a reply to a *letter of enquiry*; customarily sent with all enquiries and *unsolicited* material. (US: sase = self-addressed stamped envelope.)

standfirst: *n* an introductory *paragraph* in bigger and/or bolder *type* leading into and possibly summarising an *article*.

stanza: *n* a group of *verse* lines, usually one of a number forming a *poem*. (Italian: 'stopping place'.)

star: *n* a *symbol(1)* *, the same as an asterisk.

start page: *n* the first *web page* you see when you visit a *website*.

stat: see *photostat*.

state publishing: *n* publishing organised by a government.

stationery: *n* portable office equipment like pens, paper, envelopes *etc*.

status detail: *n* detail that reveals how *characters(1)* rank themselves or would like to be ranked in society: their possessions, clothing, cars, houses; how they treat domestic staff, waiters, colleagues; how they dress their children, which schools they send them to, *etc*.

status bar: *n* an indicator at the bottom of a computer screen showing how much of an incoming *web page* has been received.

statutory deposit copy: *n* under the 1911 Copyright Act, a copy of every *publication(2)* issued in the UK must be lodged with the British Library for registration in the *British National Bibliography*; further free copies are then requested, under legal entitlement, for distribution to The Bodleian Library at Oxford, The Library of Cambridge University, The National Library of Scotland, the National Library of Wales and The Library of Trinity College, Dublin.

stereotype: *n* a fixed idea, a *cliché*; originally, a printing plate. (Greek: 'solid type'.)

stet: *v* a *proofreader's* or *editor's* instruction meaning 'ignore marked correction'. (Latin: 'let it stand'.)

stichomythia: *n dialogue* in alternate lines, often in *verse* conveying a sense of rapid, controlled argument. (Greek: 'lines of talk'.)

sticky: *n* a *website* that attracts visitors and keeps them interested.

STM: *abbr* of *scientific, technical and medical*.

stock character: *n* a type of *character(1)* that recurs in particular *genres*, recognisable as a convention of those genres; *eg*, the plodding not-too-bright policeman who is always outsmarted by the amateur sleuth. See also *stock response, stock situation*.

stock response: *n* the predictable reaction of a *reader(1)* to a *stock character* and/or a *stock situation*; *eg*, a man wearing a dog-collar will evoke an instinctive response like 'This is a clergyman, therefore unlikely to be a *villain*'.

stock situation: *n* an often-used incident or *plot* pattern; *eg*, 'Boy meets girl, boy loses girl, boy wins girl back'.

stop press: *n* a small section in a *newspaper* reserved for very late news.

story: *n* a general term applied both to *fiction* and to news stories.

storyboard: *n* a visual prop for creating a *story*: a *bulletin board(2)* or the like on which an *author* pins plans, *character(1)* histories, descriptions, chronological sequences, *scene outlines etc*.

storyline: *n* the *plot* line, the sequence of events that keeps the action of a *story* moving forward: 'And then . . . and then . . . and next . . .'

story within a story: *n* a *story* that is actually two stories in one, the first 'framing' the telling of the second, which is usually narrated by one of the *characters(1)* in the first story and which has a *theme* complementary to the first story. See *eg* Emily Brontë's 'Wuthering Heights' (1847). Also called *frame within a frame*.

strap/strapline: *n* 1. an identification line at the top of a *manuscript* page. 2. a *subhead* appearing above a main *heading*. See also *catchline*.

strapline: see *strap*.

stream of consciousness: *n* a *narrative technique* in the form of thoughts passing through the *narrator's* mind, sometimes with little or no *punctuation*, aiming to reflect the disorganised nature of those thoughts; see *eg* James Joyce's 'Ulysses' (1922).

stringer: *n* a local *correspondent*, usually a *freelance*, who supplies *newspapers* (*regional* and/or *national*) with news from their locality.

strip cartoon: *n* a series of drawings telling a *story*.

structure: *n* the overall organisation of a work. (Latin: 'to build'.)

sturm und drang: *n* a late eighteenth-century German literary movement, exemplified by the writings of Johann Wolfgang von Goethe (1749–1832) and Johann Christoph Friedrich von Schiller (1759–1805). (German: 'Storm and stress'.)

style: *n* a distinctive way of expressing, designing or producing something. (Latin: 'writing instrument'.) See also *house style*.

style of the house: see *house style*.

style sheet: *n* a *document* giving details of *house style*, often sent to both writers and *typesetters*, to avoid the need for *style* corrections at *proof* stage.

stylist: *n* 1. a person who makes necessary minor adjustments to a *manuscript* to make it consistent with the *house style*, but who does not alter the content. 2. an advisor on the *style* and content of commissioned material.

sub: *n* 1. *abbr* of subscription. 2. a *sub-editor*.

sub-agency: *n* an agency based in a foreign country, with whom an *agent* deals when selling *foreign rights*. The sub-agent usually has a better knowledge of that country's *markets(1)* than a UK agent dealing direct, and can negotiate a better deal.

sub-edit: *v* to edit material in preparation for printing, especially in *newspapers*.

sub-editor: see under *editor*.

subgenre: *n* usually describes a niche area of *romantic fiction*, eg *romantic historical, futuristic romance, Gothic romance, Western romance, Regency romance, paranormal romance* etc.

sub-head/sub-heading: *n* 1. a brief explanatory *heading* appearing in the main body of a *text*. 2. an explanation of a main *title(1)*, printed below that title; sometimes called a *subtitle*.

subject catalogue: *n* a *catalogue* listing books according to their subject.

subjective viewpoint: *n* a *viewpoint* reflecting the personal involvement of the writer, and expressing their thoughts, feelings and opinions. Used in both *fiction* and *non-fiction*.

submission: *n* a manuscript sent to a *publisher* in the hope of *publication(1)*.

submission letter: *n* a letter accompanying a *submission* to an *agent* or *publisher*.

subplot: *n* a second *story*, complete in itself, woven into and connecting with the main story.

subscribe: *v* 1. to agree to receive and pay for something over a fixed period of time. 2. to add your name and *e-mail* address to a mailing list to receive messages from a *website*, with or without charge.

subsidiary rights: *n* a term applied to *rights* other than book rights, *eg film* and *television rights, foreign language rights, serial rights, electronic rights etc*.

subsidy publishing: *n* another term for *vanity publishing*.

subtext: *n* the situation or *theme* that underlies the action of a *story* and the behaviour of its *characters(1)*, and which might never be explained or directly referred to in the story.

subtitle: see *subhead(2)*.

success story: *n* a *non-fiction story* about people who have made a notable and perhaps unexpected success of, *eg*, an unusual career, or who have achieved success in any field against the odds.

suitability: *n* an essential quality in work intended for *publication(1)*: it must be suitable for the target *publisher*, *ie* it must have relevance to the type of material produced by that publisher.

summary: *n* a short account of the most important features of a *text(1)*. (Latin: 'the most important points'.)

superior: *n* a small *character(2)* set above the line, used mainly in mathematics or to indicate a *footnote*.

supplement: *n* 1. material added to a *publication(2)* separately, *eg* a *booklet* on hair care banded to a beauty *magazine*. 2. *matter* included in a *reprint* to add information to the original book.

surf: *v* to explore the *Internet*.

Surrealism: *n* an anti-rational and anti-realist literary and artistic movement that began in France in the 1920s.

survey article: see *round-up article*.

suspense: *n* an element in either *fiction* or *non-fiction* that builds up mental excitement, indecision or uncertainty about the eventual outcome. See also *tension*. (Latin: 'hung up'.)

suspension of disbelief: see *willing suspension of disbelief.*

swash: *n* an ornamental *character(2)*, usually a *capital letter* with flourishes.

syllabic verse: *n verse* written according to the number of *syllables* per line, rather than the number of stresses per line. See *eg* the work of the American poet Marianne Moore (1887–1972).

syllable: *n* a single sound, a part of a word.

syllepsis: *n* a *figure of speech* in which one *verb* governs two words or phrases correctly but in two different senses; *eg*, 'She walked in wearing a smile and a bathrobe'. See also *zeugma.*

symbol: *n* 1. a sign used to represent something; *eg* + for 'plus'. 2. something which signifies something else, *ie* a word or phrase suggesting other words or phrases which evoke their own references; *eg*, a cross is a symbol of Christianity and, by extension, of its history, values, influences *etc*. (Greek: 'mark', 'sign'; originally 'put together'.)

syndicate: *n* a company selling material (usually *articles* or *features*) to non-competing *publications(2)* nationwide and/or worldwide.

syndication: *n* the selling of work through a *syndicate.*

synaesthesia: *n* the mixing of sense impressions to create a particular kind of *metaphor*; *eg*, in his 'Ode to a Nightingale' (1820) John Keats describes the taste of wine thus:

> O, for a draught of vintage . . .
> Tasting of flora and the country green,
> Dance, and Provençal song, and sunburnt mirth!

combining action, sensation, colour, song and feeling. (Greek: 'feel together'.)

synecdoche: *n* a *figure of speech* in which a part is used to describe a whole (or vice versa); *eg* 'all hands on deck' in which 'hands' refers to sailors. (Greek: 'take up together'.)

synonym: *n* a word with the same meaning as another word. (Greek: 'similar name'.)

synopsis: *n* a *précis* or condensed version of the *theme* and contents of a book or *article*, giving a clear *outline* and breakdown of the proposed work. (Greek: 'view together'.)

syntax: *n* sentence structure, *ie* the way in which words and phrases are put together in order to convey the desired meaning without *ambiguity* unless ambiguity is intended. (Greek: 'arrangement'.)

T

table of contents: see *contents*.

tabloid: *n* a *newspaper* in compact *format*, usually concentrating on the more sensational and unusual aspects of current news stories.

taboo: *n* any subject, language, reference or allusion considered by a *publication(2)* to be unacceptable to its *readership*.

tabular material: *n* tables or columns of figures.

tag: *n* 1. an *HTML* command in the form of letter combinations or words surrounded by *angle brackets*, providing a hot *link(2)* to another *page* and telling a *browser* how to display that page. 2. a small decorative addition to a *character(2)*.

tagged image file format (*abbr* TIFF): a standard *file format* for storing *graphic images*.

tail margin: *n* the space between the *text(1)* and the bottom of the *page*.

tailoring: *n* the *craft* of preparing work for a specific *market(1)*, producing material in the exact *style* of a target *publication(2)*, *ie* length and complexity of words, sentences and *paragraphs*, simplicity or sophistication of language, formal or chatty style *etc*.

tailpiece: *n* a design or *illustration* at the end of a *chapter* or book.

take back: *v* an instruction to the *typesetter* to move *matter* back to the previous line or the previous *page*.

take in: *v* an instruction to the *typesetter* to include additional material provided.

take over: *v* an instruction to the *typesetter* to begin the *text(1)* on the next line rather than run it on in the same line.

tale: *n* a short *narrative* in *prose* or *verse*.

talking book: *n* a book read aloud and recorded on tape or *disk* or downloaded from a *website* so that it can be listened to.

tall story: *n* an exaggerated and unlikely *tale*.

tanka: *n* a Japanese *lyric* form consisting of thirty-one *syllables* in lines of 5/7/5/7/7 syllables. See also *haiku*.

target audience: *n* the *readers(1)*, listeners or viewers whom a work is intended to interest.

task bar: *n* the bar along the bottom of the screen that shows all currently running *programs* and open *folders*.

tautology: *n* unnecessary repetition of meaning, *eg* 'Five a.m. in the morning'. (Greek: 'saying the same'.)

teacake novel: *n* the 'Miss Marple' type of *detective fiction*, set in an English village with predominantly middle-class or upper-middle-class *characters(1)*; also called *English cosy*.

teacher's book: *n* a book designed to be used with a set of student *textbooks*, giving the teacher the answers to questions and suggestions for teaching.

team writing: *v* a team of writers, designers and *illustrators*, each of whom is usually an expert in their field, working under the direction of a supervising *editor*.

tearsheet: *n* a *page* cut ('torn') out of a *publication(2)* as 1. an example of a writer's work; 2. an example of the kind of work an *editor* wants from a writer; 3. a verification that a *piece* has been published.

teaser: *n* 1. a small *advertisement* (or a series of small ads) designed to arouse curiosity about a forthcoming product. 2, a type of *hook*, like an opening *scene* in a television play, designed to entice viewers to stay tuned to the coming production.

technical writing: *n* the writing of company and product *manuals*, reports *etc.*

technique: *n* the art and *craft* of writing, using language in the most effective way to achieve the desired result.

teleplay: *n* a *script(1)* for a play or film written especially for television.

television rights: *n* the *right* to adapt and produce a work for television.

tension: *n* the build-up of expectation, the strain (pleasurable, emotional or terrifying) of wanting to know 'what happens next', reflecting the *reader(1)'s* feelings of identification and involvement with a *character(1)'s conflict* and/or danger. See also *suspense*.

tercet: *n* a *stanza* of three lines. (Italian: 'little third'.)

terminal: *n* a processor with keyboard and screen used to access a central computer.

termination clause: *n* a *clause* determining how and when a *contract* might be ended.

territory: *n* a specification in a *contract* defining the geographic area where a *publisher* or *agent* has the right to sell a book.

tertiary level publishing: *n* publishing for education beyond secondary level.

terza rima: *n* an Italian *verse* form written in *tercets* and closing with a single line or a *couplet*; *chain-rhymed*, a terza rima can be any length. Dante's 'Divine Comedy' (*c* 1307) is written in this form. (Italian: 'third rhyme'.)

tetralogy: *n* a series of four related *plays* or *novels*. (Greek: 'four speeches'.)

tetrameter: *n* in *poetry,* a line of four *feet(2)*. (Greek: 'four measures'.)

text: 1. *n* the body of *typeset* matter in a work, as distinct from *headings, footnotes, illustrations etc*. (Latin: 'tissue'.) 2. *v* to send messages by electronic means.

text box: *n* a box within a computer *dialogue box* in which *text(1)*, dates, numbers *etc* can be entered and edited.

text CRC: *n* author-generated *camera ready copy* of *text(1)* only. (The *publisher* will add page numbers, *prelims etc*.)

textbook: *n* a book containing the main principles of a particular subject, and other material relevant to that subject; a standard book in a branch of study.

textual: *adj* relating to *text(1)*.

theatre of cruelty: *n* theatrical works in which sensational action and effects predominate and which are intended to shock the audience; *eg* Peter Weiss's play 'Marat/Sade' (1964).

theme: *n* the abstract subject of a work, the 'roots' of a *story* from which the *narrative* grows: it might examine, *eg*, a moral concept such as 'crime doesn't pay', 'love conquers all', or illustrate a specific human quality or failing, or ask a fundamental question, or look at a human problem. Not to be confused with the *plot*. (Greek: 'proposition'.)

thermoplastic binding: see *perfect binding*.

thesaurus: *n* a treasury of words, a word-finder; a systematically arranged list of words, with their *synonyms* and *antonyms*. (Greek: 'treasure'.)

thesis: *n* 1. critical or scholarly study of a work written to achieve a degree in higher education. 2. the basic argument of a work. 3. a logical proposition, intended to be countered by its *antithesis*. (Greek: 'placing'.)

third person narrative: *n* the most usual *narrative* form, telling a *story* from the *viewpoint* of one *character(1)* using the third-person 'he' or 'she' as distinct from the first-person 'I'.

thread: *n* a series of messages with a common *theme*.

threnody: *n* a lamentation, especially on someone's death. (Greek: 'wailing ode'.)

thriller: *n* a *novel*, film or play intended to arouse feelings of excitement, *tension*, and possibly fear; *eg* the *novels* of Lee Child (1954–).

throw-out: same as *fold-out*.

thumb index: *n* an *index* showing the letters of the alphabet arranged as indentations in the outer *margins* of a book.

thumbnail: *n* a small *sketch(1)*.

ticking clock effect: *n* a *technique* in *fiction* in which a time-limit is imposed on the action, to raise tension in the *narrative*.

tie-in: *n* a book or *magazine* produced to coincide with a film or television production, usually covering the same or closely related ground.

.tiff: *n* a *file* extension for a *TIFF* file.

TIFF: see *tagged image file format*.

tighten up: *v* a request or advice to a writer to cut *wordiness* and irrelevancies from a work which, apart from being flabby, is potentially publishable.

tilde: *n* the sign ~ used over the letter 'n' in Spanish to indicate the pronunciation 'ny'.

time-bomb effect: *n* an event 'planted' in a story, with the potential to 'explode' later, thus increasing tension. See *plant*.

time-line: *n* the order of events in a *story*; see *chronology*.

tip-in: *n* a single *leaf*, a *plate(2)*, or a *fold-out* inserted into a book and fixed by adhesive to the back edge of an adjoining *page*.

tip sheet: *n* a set of *guidelines*.

title: *n* 1. the identifying name by which a piece of writing or a published work is known. 2. a published or *commissioned* book.

title bar: *n* a horizontal bar at the top of a computer screen showing the name of the *program* and *file* currently in use.

title page: *n* the *recto page* following the *half-title verso*, bearing the *title(1)* of the book, the *author's* name, sometimes the *publisher's* name and/or *colophon(1)*, and other relevant data.

title verso: *n* the *page* backing the *title page*, usually carrying *copyright* data, *publisher's* address, *ISBN*, *typesetting* and printing data, and the book's publishing history. See *bibliographic page*.

tone: *n* the over-all effect achieved by your writing *technique* and choice of words, and your attitude to the subject.

toolbar: *n* a row of screen *icons* to guide you in using a word processing or *browser program*.

topic: *n* a subject, a *theme* for discussion. (Greek: 'place'.)

topical: *adj* of current interest.

tract: *n* a short *essay* or *pamphlet* on a controversial subject, usually political or religious. (Latin: 'treatment'.)

trade book: *n* a book produced for general retail sale through bookshops, as distinct from *book clubs* or mass market outlets.

trade discount: *n* a discount on the *cover price*, granted to a *bookseller* by a *publisher*.

trade edition: *n* an *edition* of a book intended for sale through retailers, as distinct from an edition produced for *book clubs* or the education market.

trade house: *n* a printing company which works mainly for other printers.

trade journal: *n* a *periodical* produced for circulation among practitioners and companies in a particular trade or industry, *eg* 'The Grocer', 'House Builder'.

trade mark: *n* a name, sign or *symbol(1)* printed on something to identify its maker.

trade paperback: *n* an 'up-market' *paperback*, more elegantly produced than most standard paperbacks, often with heavier and more ornate covers.

tragedy: *n* a dramatic or literary work in which the main *protagonist* suffers sorrow or ruin, usually because of moral weakness, an inherent flaw, or an inability to cope with a situation; *eg* Hamlet's tragedy sprang from an inherent inability to make up his mind. (Greek: 'goat song'.)

tragicomedy: *n* a mixture of *tragedy* and *comedy*; *eg* Shakespeare's 'The Winter's Tale' (1610).

transgressive fiction: *n* the exploration in *fiction* of *taboos*, based on the belief that knowledge is to be found at the edge of experience; see *eg* the work of William Burroughs (1914–97).

transition: *n* 1. a connecting link between divisions of thought, a 'bridge' that invites you to carry on reading through a shift from one idea to another; *eg* 'Let's leave that and turn to . . .', 'On the other hand . . .'. 2. a passage leading from one *scene(2)* to the next.

translation rights: *n* the *right* to publish a book in a language other than the language in which it was first published.

transparency: *n* a photograph on slide film rather than in negative or digital form.

transpose (*abbr* trs): *v* to change the order of letters, words, lines *etc*.

travel guide: *n* a book giving tourist information about a place, such as how to get there, where to stay and what to see.

travel magazine: *n* a *magazine* publishing *articles* about holidays and travel.

travel writing: *n* writing that is about places visited, giving *facts*, impressions and insights into those places and the people who live there.

treatise: *n* a systematic and careful examination of a subject.

treatment: *n* an *outline* written by a *scriptwriter* as a preliminary to the full *script*, emphasising the intended *style* and approach, and sometimes including key *dialogue*.

trilogy: *n* a group of three connected literary works. (Greek: 'three speeches'.)

trimeter: *n* a line consisting of three *feet(2)*. (Greek: 'three measure'.)

triolet: *n* a short poetic form of eight lines, rhyming scheme ABaAabAB. (French: 'little three'.)

triple rhyme: *n* a *rhyme* on three *syllables*, *eg* 'quivering/shivering'; mostly used for comic effect.

triplet: *n* a *stanza* of three similar or rhyming lines.

trivia: *pl n* insignificant items, details or information.

trochee: *n* in *verse*, a *foot(2)* consisting of a stressed *syllable* followed by a weaker syllable. (Greek: 'running'.)

trojan: *n* a computer *virus* that disguises itself as an innocent *program*.

trs: *abbr* of *transpose*.

true confessions: see *confession story*.

true crime writing: *n non-fiction* accounts of real crimes, possibly dramatising how they were committed and solved.

ts: see *typescript*.

turnaround time: *n* the time specified for a particular job to be done, *eg* for an *author* to read, correct and return *proofs*.

tweet: 1. *n* a message sent via *Twitter*. 2. *v* to send a message via *Twitter*.

twist in the tail story: *n* a *story* in which the ending is a surprise but nonetheless a logical conclusion.

Twitter: *n* a free-to-use *social networking* tool for displaying and sending very short messages (140 *characters(2)* maximum) called *tweets* via computer or mobile phone.

type: *n characters(2)*, *numerals*, signs *etc* used in printing, formerly made from wood or metal but nowadays most commonly reproduced by computer technology.

typeface: *n* a particular design of *type*. Each typeface, whether appearing in *roman*, *italic*, *bold* or another variation, has design characteristics that distinguish it from other typefaces.

typescript (*abbr* ts): *n* a typewritten *manuscript*.

typeset: *n* and *v*; put into *type*.

typesetter: *n* a person (or company) who *sets type*.

typesetting: v the process of converting *copy* into a form in which it can be used for printing; also called *setting*.

type specimen sheet: *n* a printed sheet showing examples of different *typefaces* and the various forms (*roman*, *italic*, *bold etc*) in which they are available.

typo (US): *n* a *literal*.

typographer: *n* a designer of printed material.

typographical error (US typo): see *literal*.

typography: *n* the art of designing printed *matter* by selecting appropriate *typefaces*, *type* sizes and *layouts*.

U

uc: see *upper case*.

umlaut: *n* a pronunciation indicator of two dots above a vowel, *eg* ü, especially in German.

unabridged: *adj* not shortened or condensed.

unagented: *adj* describes an *author* or a *submission* not represented by an *agent*.

unattributed: *adj* not attributed to any source or creator.

unauthorised biography: see *biography*.

unauthorised edition: *n* a pirated *edition* not authorised by the *publisher*.

unbacked: *n* printed on one side of the paper only.

under contract: *adj* bound by the terms of a *contract*.

underline: 1. *n* a *caption*. 2. *v* an instruction to the *typesetter* that specific material indicated in the *typescript* should be underlined, not *set* in *italics*.

underlining: *n* a system used by *editors* to indicate different *type* styles; single underlining means 'set in *italics*', double underlining means 'set in *small caps*', triple underlining means 'set in *caps*', wavy underlining means 'set in *bold*'.

understatement: *n* deliberate restraint of expression, presenting something as being less important than it really is.

unearned advance: *n* money received as *royalties* but not yet covered by the royalties earned from sales.

unexpurgated: *adj* not having had offensive or unsuitable material removed.

uniform edition: *n* a set of books in an identical design.

Uniform Resource Locator (*abbr* URL): *n* a web-addressing system that identifies an *Internet document's* type and location.

unique selling point (*abbr* USP): *n* a quality that makes a product or service different from and/or better than its rivals.

unit cost: *n* the production cost per copy of a project, calculated by adding the *fixed costs* and *running costs* then dividing by the *print run*; the cost on which the selling price is based.

Universal Serial Bus (*abbr* USB): *n* one of a range of easy-to-use connections allowing you to connect devices to your computer.

university press: *n* a *publisher* directly or indirectly associated with a university.

unjustified setting: *n* *matter* not *set* in lines of equal length, but not exceeding a specified *measure*, thus giving a *ragged right* edge.

unlawful copying: *n* the copying of material without the consent of the *copyright* holder.

unleaded: *adj* having no white space (*leading*) between lines of *type*.

unpaged: *adj* having no *page* numbers.

unpublishable: *adj* not suitable for publishing in any form by anyone.

unpublished: *adj* not having been published.

unreliable narrator: *n* in *fiction*, a *narrator* whose truthfulness can't be trusted.

unsolicited submission: *n* work sent to an *editor* or *publisher* entirely *on spec* and without invitation, in the hope that they will take it on. See also *on speculation*.

untitled: *adj* having no *title*.

update: *v* to *edit* by adding current data or altering out-of-date information.

upload: *v* to send *files* from a computer to a *host* via the *Internet*.

upper case (*abbr* uc): *n capital letters*. So called because in the days when *type* was *set* by hand, the capitals were kept in a separate case situated above the *lower case* which held the small letters.

urban legend: *n* a *story* that is almost invariably untrue, but which circulates persistently by word of mouth.

URL: see *Uniform Resource Locator*.

USB: see *Universal Serial Bus*.

USP: See *unique selling point*.

usual rates: *n* the usual rates of payment offered by a *publication(2)* to *freelance* writers. Some pay higher rates to established writers than to those as yet unknown.

user's manual: *n* a *guide* showing how to use something.

Utopia: *n.* the ideal political state and way of life; from the book *Utopia* (1515–16) by Sir Thomas More. (Greek: outopia = 'no place' and eutopia = 'good place'.)

V

valediction: *n* a farewell speech. (Latin: 'saying farewell'.)

validator: *n* a *website* that validates *HTML* codes.

vanity publishing: *n* a business arrangement whereby an *author* pays a company to publish their work. Not to be confused with *self-publishing*, where the author acts as their own *publisher*. For more information, see http://www.vanitypublishing.info/, the *website* of Johnathon Clifford, who campaigns against the exploitation of authors.

vaporlink: *n* a *link(2)* that points to a non-existent *web page*.

variable cost: *n* a cost that increases with the volume of goods produced, *eg* wages and materials.

variorum edition: *n* an *edition* of a work which includes the observations of different commentators and/or textual variations of that work in *manuscripts* and subsequent editions. (Latin: 'of various'.)

VDU: see *visual display unit*.

vegetable soup: *n* a derogatory term describing writing that is put together in a haphazard and disorganised way.

verb: *n* a word or group of words signifying an action.

verbal sketch: *n* the writer's version of the artist's on-the-spot *sketch(1)*, *ie* the immediate noting down of something striking, such as a *location*, a *character(1)*, a snatch of conversation *etc*, with a view to working it up later.

verbatim: *n* a Latin term meaning 'in exactly the same words'.

verbiage: *n* the same as *wordiness*.

verification: *n* the thorough checking and authentication of *facts*, information, *quotations etc*.

verisimilitude: *n* having the appearance of truth or reality. (Latin: 'like the truth'.)

vernacular: *n* the language of one's homeland; often used to describe *dialect*. (Latin: 'domestic', 'indigenous'.)

vers libre: *n* French for *free verse*.

verse: *n* metrical lines of *poetry*. (Latin: 'turn of the plough'.)

versification: *n* the study of the art of writing *verse*, or the act of writing verse.

verso page: *n* the left-hand *page* of an open book, usually with even numbers. (Latin: 'turned'.)

vetting: *n* the examination and investigation of a *manuscript* by an expert in the work's subject.

vide: *v* a Latin word meaning 'see', used to direct a *reader(1)* to another part of a *text(1)*; *eg* 'vide infra' (see below), 'vide supra' (see above).

viewpoint: *n* the point of view from which a *story* or *article* is told; the selected position of the *author*. See *detached viewpoint, multiple viewpoint, objective viewpoint,* *omniscient viewpoint, subjective viewpoint.*

viewpoint character: *n* the *character(1)* from whose *viewpoint* a *story* is told, and through whose thoughts, emotions, actions and reactions the story is shown.

vignette: *n* a brief *verbal sketch* or *anecdote* offering a flash of illumination about a *character(1)* or situation. (French: 'small vine'.)

villain: *n* a *character(1)* who is the focus of evil. (French: 'feudal serf'.)

villanelle: *n* a nineteen-line *poem* consisting of five *tercets* and a final *quatrain* using only two *rhymes*; the first and third lines of the first tercet repeat alternately as a *refrain* closing the succeeding *stanzas* and join as the final *couplet* of the quatrain. See *eg* Dylan Thomas's 'Do not go gentle into that good night . . .' (1951). (Italian: 'rustic'.)

virgule: *n* the stroke /; see also *solidus, slash.*

visual: *n* a *layout* or *rough* of *artwork.*

visual display unit (*abbr* VDU): *n* a cathode ray tube on which the output of a computer can be shown.

viz: *adv abbr* of the Latin word 'videlicet', meaning 'namely'; used to specify examples or items.

vocabulary: *n* the number of words in a specific language, or related to a particular subject.

vogue word: *n* a word which comes into fashion, is used to excess, then quickly loses popularity. See also *buzz word.*

voice: *n* the distinctive *style* and *tone* which distinguish one writer's work from that of others. See also *active voice, passive voice.*

voice over internet protocol (*abbr* VOIP): *n* the making of phone calls via the *Internet* rather than via a standard telephone line.

void: *adj* not legally valid.

VOIP: see *Voice Over Internet Protocol.*

volume: *n* a bound book; applied especially to one book from a multiple-volume set.

volume discount: *n* a discount given for buying in bulk.

volume rights: *n* the *right* of a *publisher* to produce and publish a work in all *editions* in specified parts of the world during the full term of *copyright*, and to publish other editions and to lease publishing rights to another publisher.

voucher copy: *n* a copy of a single *issue* of a *publication(2)* sent free by the *publisher* to a writer whose work appears in that issue, as evidence (to vouch) that the work has been published. Not obligatory, but many publishers observe this courtesy.

W

waiver clause: *n* a *clause* in a *contract* defining the conditions under which specified *rights* can be given up.

wake-up start: *n* an over-used *story* opening showing the main *character(1)* waking up in the morning, and following them in tedious detail through a chronological sequence of trivial events, thoughts, actions *etc.*

war poet: *n* describes a *poet* who wrote about the First World War; *eg* Rupert Brooke (1887–1915), Robert Graves (1895–1985).

warranty: *n* a guarantee signed by the *author* to indemnify the *publisher* against any legal action arising from the contents of a book. Warranty and *indemnity clauses* vary from *contract* to contract.

warts: *n* distinguishing characteristics, not necessarily attractive, that make a *character(1)* memorable; can be physical or psychological.

Watson: *n* a detective's 'side-kick'; derives from Dr. Watson, Sherlock Holmes's associate, whose less than successful attempts at crime-solving were designed to make Holmes's skill and analytical powers look even more brilliant. Famous Watsons include Hercule Poirot's Captain Hastings, Nero Wolfe's Archie Goodwin and Inspector Morse's Sergeant Lewis.

WCT: See *WIPO Copyright Treaty*.

web: *n abbr* of the *World Wide Web*.

web crawler: *n* a *program* that searches through *web pages* for a specific word, phrase or topic.

web folio: *n* a collection of *web pages* with a defining *theme*.

web server: *n* a *program* that locates and 'serves up' *web pages* as you request them.

webcam: *n* a camera that lets you make video calls via the *Internet*.

webcasting: *v* using the *World Wide Web* as a means of broadcasting information.

weblog: see *blog*.

webmaster: *n* someone who creates, organises or updates information on a *website*.

web page: *n* a computer *file* accessible through the *World Wide Web*.

webring: *n* a collection of related *websites* using special *links(2)* to connect one site to another.

website: *n* an *Internet* location set up by individuals or companies to promote themselves, their works and their services.

weekly: *n* a *publication(2)* that is produced every week.

western: *n* can be *fiction* or *non-fiction*, but usually refers to a *genre* of *novel* defined by the Western Writers of America as a *story* set in the American West (the 'Wild West') before the 20th century.

western romance: *n* a *subgenre* of *romantic fiction*, describing *stories* set in the American West (see *western*) and sometimes in the Canadian West.

wf: *n abbr* of 'wrong *fount*', used in *proof* correction.

'What you see is what you get': the full form of WYSIWYG.

white line: *n* a line of blank paper, the depth of a line of *type*.

white space: *n* the parts of a printed *page* where no printing appears.

who-dun-it?: *n* a classic form of *detective fiction*, in which the identity of the villain is not revealed till the end.

'who, what, why, where and when': *n* the five 'w's of *journalism*, essential to full coverage of a *topic*.

why-dun-it?: *n* a formula for many psychological mystery stories. The criminal's identity is revealed early in the story, possibly at the beginning, and the interest lies in tracing the reasons and motives for the crime.

widow: *n* a short last line of a *paragraph* appearing as the first line of the next *page* or *column(1)*; typographically undesirable.

Wi-Fi: *n* computer networking technology that allows data to be transferred via radio waves; *abbr* of *Wireless-Fidelity*.

wiki: *n* a type of *website* designed to be added to or edited by its users; *eg* the *online encyclopaedia* 'Wikipedia'. (Hawaiian: 'fast'.)

willing suspension of disbelief: *n* a willingness on the part of the *reader(1)* to accept as true, while reading, something they would normally find hard to believe.

window: *n* a section of a computer screen.

WIPO: see *World Intellectual Property Organization*.

WIPO Copyright Treaty: *n* a set of guidelines regarding *copyright* protection on *software* and *databases*, as well as technology relating to copyright, *eg* anti-copying devices on *compact disks*; came into force in the EU in 2002.

Wireless-Fidelity: see *Wi-Fi*.

wizard: *n* a feature within an *application* that shows you, step-by-step, how to perform a particular task.

women's: *n* a category of literature whose subjects are specifically related to the interests, needs and aspirations of contemporary women.

word break: *n* a division of a word by a hyphen at the end of a line.

word count: *n* the number of words in a piece of writing.

word music: *n* the sounds that words and combinations of words evoke in the *reader(1)'s* mind and emotions, setting the *tone* and *mood*, and manipulating their responses.

word pictures: *n* the images that words 'paint' in the *reader(1)'s* mind.

word processing program: *n* a *program* using computer logic to accept, store and retrieve material for editing and printing out on paper or storing on the computer's *hard drive* or on removable computer *software*.

word space: *n* variable space between words.

wordage: *n* the length of a *text(1)* expressed as a *word count*.

wordiness: *n* the use of unnecessary words, almost invariably to the detriment of the writing's quality: an excess of *adjectives*, *adverbs*, *conjunctions*, descriptive phrases, *tautology*, irrelevancies *etc*.

work in progress: *n* 1. whatever a writer is currently working on. 2. in *publishers'* terms, those books currently in production.

work station: *n* a desk with a computer and *keyboard*, and possibly a printer.

workbook: *n* a book made up of problems to be solved, usually supplementing an educational *publication(2)* and sometimes designed to be written in.

working title: *n* an identifying name given to a *work in progress*, not necessarily the final *title(1)*.

workshop: *n* a group of people meeting to write and to exchange opinions and constructive suggestions on current work, usually under the guidance of a writer/tutor. See also *writers' circle*.

World Intellectual Property Organization (*abbr* **WIPO**): *n* an agency of the United Nations dedicated to developing a balanced and accessible international intellectual property system which rewards creativity, stimulates innovation and contributes to economic development while safeguarding the public interest.

World Wide Web (*abbr* **www**): *n* a network of graphic and *text(1) document* 'pages' linked together electronically on the *Internet*. Also called 'the web'.

worm: *n* a type of *virus* that can spread via the *Internet* or a *network* without the need to attach itself to a *document*.

wrap-round: *n* a small group of *pages*, often *illustrations*, placed outside a *signature*, so that half the group comes before the signature and half after it.

writer in residence: *n* an experienced writer employed for a set period to teach, guide and encourage *creative writing* in a variety of institutions such as colleges, further education centres, libraries, prisons, rehabilitation centres *etc.*

writer's block: *n* the psychological inability to begin a piece of writing or to continue with a *work in progress*.

writers' circle: *n* a group of people meeting to read, discuss and possibly criticise each other's work; differs from a *workshop* in that the work is usually done at home beforehand instead of being at least partly done during the meeting.

writers' guidelines: see *guidelines*.

Writers' Guild of Great Britain, The: *n* a trade union affiliated to the Trades Union Congress representing the interests of writers, especially those working in theatre, radio, film and television, books and the new *media*; see www.writersguild.org.uk.

writers' magazine: *n* a *magazine* devoted to the interests of writers, both novices and the more experienced, giving advice, instruction, inspiration and information about all aspects of writing and getting published; *eg* 'Writing Magazine', 'Writers' News', 'Writers' Forum' in the UK and 'Writer's Digest' and 'The Writer' in the USA.

Writer's Room, The: see *BBC Writer's Room*.

writers' seminar: *n* a meeting lasting at least a few hours, but could be a whole day, a weekend, or even a week, with discussions, possibly *workshops*, courses and advice sessions, displays of books and *magazines*, and probably experienced writers as guest speakers. Offers valuable opportunities to meet and talk with other writers.

writing services: *n* services supplied by *freelances* for the production of material, especially for publicity and training programmes.

wrong fount (*abbr* **wf**): *n* a correction mark showing the printer that a *character(2)* is *set* in the wrong *fount*.

www: see *World Wide Web*.

WYSIWYG: *n acronym* of 'What you see is what you get'.

X

XML: see *Extensible Markup Language*.

Y

yarn: *n* an informal term for a *story*, mainly *adventure* or *western*, in which the *storyline* is long, possibly rambling, and packed with action and incident.

yearbook: *n* an annual *publication(2)* reviewing the past year's events and/or updating information about its area of interest.

yellow press: see *gutter press*.

young adult: *n* a *category* of writing for *readers(1)* aged about twelve to seventeen.

Z

zeitgeist: *n* the spirit of an age or period. (German: 'time spirit'.)

zeugma: *n* a *figure of speech* in which the same *verb* or *adjective* is applied to two *nouns* of different meaning; *eg* 'Miss Bolo rose from the table considerably agitated, and went straight home, in a flood of tears, and a sedan chair.' (Charles Dickens, 'The Pickwick Papers' (1836–7). (Greek: 'yoking'.) See also *syllepsis*.

zip file: *n* a computer *file* with the extension '.zip' containing data that is compressed for speedier transmission.

.zip: *n* a *file* extension for a *zip file*.

zine: *n* a specialist *publication(2)*, usually produced by an individual or a *small press*, aimed at a specialist *readership*.

zoom: *n* a facility enabling the visible but not actual enlargement or contraction of material on screen.

Writing 'how-to' articles and books:

How to share your know-how and get published

Writers' Guides: A Studymates Series

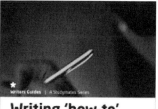

Author
Chriss McCallum
Price
£10.99

Format
Paperback, 215 x 135 mm, 240pp
ISBN 13
978-1-84285-095-4

About the author
Chriss McCallum worked for Collins Publishing for many years, first as an editor and then in book production. She is a published writer and has taught creative writing, as well as publishing her own magazines for writers. Chriss lives in Cheshire with her husband.

Writers' Guides: A Studymates Series

Here is how to use the knowledge you have, to help others and become a published writer yourself.

In this book Chriss McCallum explains how to:
- Assess your knowledge and experience.
- Write 'how-to' articles.
- Write for magazines.
- Survive and succeed in today's publishing world.
- Break in with tips and fillers.
- Approach your market.
- Write a 'how-to' book.

Market
All students taking courses to improve their writing skills
- Post 16-Level students and first-year undergraduates on publishing and other related writing studies/degrees.
- Adult education centres including WEA.
- Teachers, tutors and lecturers.
- School libraries, reference and public libraries.
- University and college central libraries.

SUBJECT AREA
English Language/Creative Writing/Publishing

Related Titles
Writing TV Scripts 978-1-84285-071-8
Writing Historical Fiction 978-1-84285-077-0
Starting to Write 978-184285-093-0
Writing Crime 978-1-84285-088-6
12-Point Guide to Writing Romance 978-1-84285-131-9